ABOUT THE
STARMONT READER'S GUIDES TO CONTEMPORARY
SCIENCE FICTION AND FANTASY AUTHORS

The past two decades have seen an enormous upsurge in the interest in science fiction and fantasy. It is rare to find a bookstore that doesn't now prominently feature brightly colored examples of space and magic. It is unusual to find a high school, college, or university that doesn't offer at least one science fiction or fantasy course. Most significantly, it is becoming increasingly difficult to meet someone who hasn't succumbed to the lure of these two entertaining literatures. The Starmont Reader's Guides were created to satisfy the needs and interests of this varied readership. Bringing together acknowledged authorities, the series offers a thorough examination of each author; indeed, many of these efforts represent the first time the authors have been examined in book form. Each volume is divided into a chronological table of the author's life and literary career, a full biography, chapters on the major works or groups of works, and both primary and secondary bibliographies. Without sacrificing the sophistication that each author creates in his or her fiction, they clearly and cogently explore and explain the important issues, providing depth and understanding for both the beginning and the sophisticated reader.

It is hoped that the Starmont Reader's Guides will be of value to the student, teacher, librarian, scholar and fan by contributing to our understanding of the many authors and fascinating works that have provided us all with so much pleasure and insight.

Dr. Roger C. Schlobin, Series Editor

DR. ROGER C. SCHLOBIN is currently an Associate Professor of English at the North Central Campus of Purdue University. He is co-editor of "The Year's Scholarship in Science Fiction and Fantasy," which appears annually in *Extrapolation*; one of the authors of *A Research Guide to Science Fiction Studies*; and has written *The Literature of Fantasy: An Annotated Bibliography of Fantasy-Fiction* as well as the bibliography of the works of Andre Norton.

arthur c. clarke

STARMONT READER'S GUIDE 1
ERIC S. RABKIN
Series Editor: ROGER C. SCHLOBIN

STARMONT HOUSE
P.O. Box 851   Mercer Island, Washington 98040

For

Betsy
Donnie
Gary
Matt
Sue

Library of Congress Catalog Card Number: 79-84709
ISBN: 0-916732-21-5

Cover by Stephen Fabian

Revised, Second Edition, 1980

DR. ERIC S. RABKIN is a Professor of English at the University of Michigan. Among his numerous publications are *Narrative Suspense*; *Form in Fiction*; *The Fantastic in Literature*; and *Science Fiction: History, Science, Vision*.

CONTENTS

ABBREVIATIONS

Because popular fiction goes in and out of print so rapidly and because standard editions are non-existent and first editions often rare, in this volume citation is made whenever possible not to page numbers but to chapters. To make these citations as unobtrusive as possible, they occur parenthetically in the text and use the following system of abbreviations:

AFN   *Against the Fall of Night*
CE   *Childhood's End*
CS   *The City and the Stars*
DI   *Dolphin Island*
DR   *The Deep Range*
EE   *Expedition to Earth*
EL   *Earthlight*
FM   *A Fall of Moondust*
FOP   *The Fountains of Paradise*
GP   *Glide Path*
IE   *Imperial Earth*
IS   *Islands in the Sky*
LC   *The Lion of Comarre*
LW   *The Lost Worlds of 2001*
NBN   *The Nine Billion Names of God*
OSS   *The Other Side of the Sky*
PS   *Prelude to Space*
RFT   *Reach For Tomorrow*
RWR   *Rendezvous With Rama*
SM   *The Sands of Mars*
TTW   *Tales of Ten Worlds*
TWH   *Tales From the "White Hart"*
2001 *2001: A Space Odyssey*
WFS   *The Wind From The Sun*

CHRONOLOGY OF LIFE AND WORKS

One of the most influential writers and scientific speculators of our age, Arthur Charles Clarke has produced a body of writings, numbering well over five hundred items, that has provoked and delighted and stirred a world-wide readership of all ages and levels of education. Included among his many fine works of fiction are *Childhood's End,* a novel of the transcendence of the human race which is perhaps the single most studied book of science fiction, and "The Nine Billion Names of God," a short story of science and religion in confrontation which the Science Fiction Writers of America have chosen as one of the most important stories of all time. He has won every major science fiction award. His vast output of non-fiction exposition and speculation has gained him international recognition as a scientific authority and conspicuous opportunities as a commentator on and a collaborator with those who are conquering space in fact. Clarke's scientific writing has been honored with every major award in its field. His collaboration with Mike Wilson in undersea exploration has led to the writing of books, the publication of biological and archaeological papers, and the production of films and television shows. Intense work with Stanley Kubrick eventuated in the co-authored screenplay for *2001: A Space Odyssey,* arguably the most important science fiction film of all time, and Clarke's own novelization, itself a masterpiece in the traditions of Wells and Stapledon. This guide concentrates on Clarke's fiction, giving fullest treatment to his most important works and descriptions of most of the remainder, but any attempt to understand the importance of this body of fiction and to properly understand its sources requires at least an outline knowledge of Clarke's exceptionally active life. The following chronology provides that outline. In addition, all of his books are listed here so that the integration among science, science fiction and the writing about these subjects that has been maintained throughout a long and honored career can be seen.

1917   Born in Minehead, Somerset, England on the Bristol Channel on 16 Dec; son of Charles Wright Clarke and Norah Mary Willis Clarke.
1927-36   Educated at Huish's Grammar School, Taunton, Somerset.
1929   Began to read science fiction, first in Hugo Gernsback's *Amazing Stories* and then from the library, especially concentrating on H. G. Wells and Rudyard Kipling.

1931   Read Olaf Stapledon's *Last and First Men* (1930): "The book transformed my life."

1935   Joined the British Interplanetary Society, a group of adult scientific amateurs founded in Liverpool in 1933.

1936-41   Being excellent in mathematics but not having the funds for higher education, he tested for and easily placed in the civil service examinations, securing the post of Assistant Auditor, His Majesty's Exchequer and Audit Department.

1937   Began publishing short science fiction in *Novae Terrae*, a fan magazine he and friends put out on mimeograph.

1941-46   Royal Air Force. Although his job at the Exchequer was a reserved occupation, he chose to enlist. Myopia kept him out of the air, but he attended electronics school, radar school, and eventually became a radar instructor, mustering out as Flight Lieutenant.

1943   Technical Officer on the experimental trials of the first GCA (Ground Controlled Approach) radar, the invention of Nobel Laureate Luis Alvarez.

1945   Originated communications satellites in a technical paper, "Extraterrestrial Relays," published in the October issue of the engineering journal, *Wireless World*.

1946   Entered King's College, London, on a grant.

"Loophole," Clarke's first professional fiction publication, appeared in the April *Astounding Science Fiction*.

"Rescue Party," which Clarke considers his "first published story," because it was written in 1945, appeared in the May *Astounding Science Fiction*.

1946-47   Chairman, British Interplanetary Society.

1948   B.Sc. (1st Class Honours) in physics and mathematics.

1949-50   Assistant Editor of *Science Abstracts*, a technical journal published by the Institute of Electrical Engineers.

1950   *Interplanetary Flight: An Introduction to Astronautics* (nonfiction).

1951   *Prelude to Space* (novel).

The Sands of Mars (novel).

The Exploration of Space (non-fiction); Book-of-the-Month Club selection.

1952   International Fantasy Award for non-fiction for *The Exploration of Space*.

Islands in the Sky (novel).

1953   Married Marilyn Mayfield.

Against the Fall of Night (novel), written between 1937 and 1946, and first published in the November 1948 *Startling Stories*.

Childhood's End (novel).
Expedition to Earth (short stories).

1954   Engaged in underwater exploration on Great Barrier Reef of Australia and in the coastal waters of Sri Lanka (formerly Ceylon).

1954   *Going Into Space* (non-fiction).
The Exploration of the Moon (non-fiction), with R. A. Smith.

1955   *Earthlight* (novel).

1956   Moved permanent residence to Sri Lanka.
Hugo Award for "The Star."
The City and the Stars (novel).
Reach For Tomorrow (short stories).
The Coast of Coral (non-fiction).

1957   *The Deep Range* (novel).
Tales From The "White Hart" (short stories).
The Making of a Moon: The Story of the Earth Satellite Program (non-fiction); revised edition, 1958.
The Reefs of Taprobane: Underwater Adventures Around Ceylon (non-fiction).

1958   *The Other Side of the Sky* (short stories).
Voice Across the Sea (non-fiction).
Boy Beneath the Sea (non-fiction), with Mike Wilson.

1959   *Across the Sea of Stars* (collection including two novels and eighteen short stories).
The Challenge of the Spaceship: Previews of Tomorrow's World (non-fiction).

1960   *The Challenge of the Sea* (non-fiction).
The First Five Fathoms: A Guide to Underwater Adventure (non-fiction), with Mike Wilson.

1961   UNESCO Kalinga Prize for science writing (£1000).
Elected Fellow of the Academy of Astronautics.
Boys' Clubs of America Junior Book Award.
A Fall of Moondust (novel).
Indian Ocean Adventure (non-fiction), with Mike Wilson.

1962   Elected to World Academy of Art and Science.
Tales of Ten Worlds (short stories).
From the Ocean, From the Stars (collection including two novels and twenty-four short stories).
Profiles of the Future: An Inquiry into the Limits of the Possible (non-fiction).

1963   Stuart Ballantine Medal of the Franklin Institute for originating communications satellites.
Dolphin Island (novel).

Glide Path (novel).
1964 Divorced.
The Treasure of the Great Reef (non-fiction), with Mike Wilson.
Indian Ocean Treasure (non-fiction), with Mike Wilson.
Man and Space (non-fiction), with the editors of *Life*.
1965 Robert Ball Award of the Aviation-Space Writers' Association for journalism for a *Life* article on communications satellites.
Prelude to Mars (collection including two novels and sixteen short stories).
Voices From the Sky: Previews of the Coming Age (non-fiction).
1966 *Time Probe: The Science in Science Fiction* (fiction by others edited by Clarke).
1967 *The Nine Billion Names of God* (collection of twenty-five short stories).
The Coming of the Space Age: Famous Accounts of Man's Probing of the Universe (non-fiction edited by Clarke).
1968 *2001: A Space Odyssey* (screenplay), with Stanley Kubrick.
2001: A Space Odyssey (novel).
The Lion of Commare, and Against the Fall of Night (the former novel was written in 1946, first published in August 1949 *Thrilling Wonder Stories).*
The Promise of Space (non-fiction).
1969 Westinghouse-American Association for the Advancement of Science Writing Award.
Oscar nomination with Kubrick for *2001* screenplay.
1970 *First on the Moon* (non-fiction), with the Apollo 11 astronauts.
1972 *The Wind From The Sun* (short stories).
The Lost Worlds of 2001 (memoirs, comments and fiction relating to *2001).*
Report on Planet Three (non-fiction).
Beyond Jupiter (non-fiction), with the artist Chesley Bonestell.
Into Space (non-fiction), with Robert Silverberg.
1973 *Rendezvous With Rama* (novel).
The Best of Arthur C. Clarke (short stories).
1974 American Institute of Aeronautics and Astronautics Aerospace Communications Award.
Nebula, Hugo and John W. Campbell Awards for *Rendezvous With Rama.*
1976 *Imperial Earth* (novel).
1977 *The View From Serendip* (non-fiction).
Bradford Washburn Award for contributions to the public understanding of science.
1979 *The Fountains of Paradise* (novel).

BIO-CRITICAL INTRODUCTION

The great line of British science fiction runs from Herbert George Wells (1866-1946) to William Olaf Stapledon (1886-1950) to Arthur Charles Clarke (1917-   ). While admitting the enormous influence on his own work of the two earlier writers, both of whom are deeply philosophical in their fictions, Clarke nonetheless modestly refers to himself "primarily as an entertainer" (Contemporary Novelists, Ed. James Vinson). That he is entertaining there can be no doubt: while new science fiction books come into print and go out again faster than even a devoted fan can follow, all of Clarke's novels are in print, and some, like Childhood's End, have been continuously available for a quarter of a century. By this standard of popularity alone, it should be clear that Clarke is no "mere" entertainer. His unique combination of strong plots of discovery and compelling scientific detail mark his work as among the most polished in the genre. But what truly distinguishes Clarke's fictions from the usually more ephemeral examples of science fiction is his vision, a humane and open and fundamentally optimistic view of humankind and its potential in a universe which dwarfs us in physical size but which we may hope some day to match in spirit.

> I came across [Olaf Stapledon's Last and First Men] in the public library of my birthplace, Minehead, soon after its first appearance in 1930. With its multimillion-year vistas, and its roll call of great but doomed civilizations, the book produced an overwhelming impact upon me. I can still remember patiently copying Stapledon's "Time Scales"—up to the last one, where "Planets Formed" and "End of Man" lie only a fraction of an inch on either side of the moment marked "Today" (LC, Introduction).

Stapledon, who wrote philosophical treatises and worked as an extramural lecturer in philosophy, explicitly revealed his purpose in using science fiction:

> To romance of the far future, then, is to attempt to see the human race in its cosmic setting, and to mould our hearts to entertain new values (Last and First Men, Preface to the English edition).

Apparently the young Clarke's heart was open to moulding. Indeed, in Prelude to Space, a troubled character wanders through Hyde Park, fa-

13

mous for its soap-box speakers, noting how one form of silliness succeeds another until finally his attention is arrested by

> an elderly, white-haired man . . . giving . . . a remarkably well--informed lecture—on philosophy. [He] might have been a retired schoolmaster with such strong views on adult education that he felt compelled to hold forth in the marketplace to all who would listen.
>
> His discourse was on Life, its origin and destiny . . . he began to speak of the astronomical stage upon which the strange drama of life was being played.
>
> . . . though Dirk was not sure that he confined himself to accepted scientific knowledge, the general impression he gave was accurate enough *(PS,* chapter 7).

This obvious homage to Stapledon has an almost Shakespearean ring, recalling both in situation and phrasing the famous lines of *As You Like It* (II, vii, 11, 139-166), beginning "All the world's a stage," lines that encompass the whole career of a person from birth to death. The "astronomical stage" allows for a dramatic juxtaposition of "scales," like Stapledon's "Time Scales," to put humanity into new perspectives so that we may see "truths and beauties which, though implicit in . . . experience, would otherwise be overlooked" (*Last and First Men,* chapter 16, part 2). Shakespeare himself offers one of the great expressions of this confrontation of scales:

> As flies to wanton boys, are we to the gods—
> They kill us for their sport (*King Lear,* IV, i, 11. 36-37).

Wells used precisely the same rhetorical technique on the opening page of *The War of the Worlds* (1898):

> . . . across the gulf of space, minds that are to our minds as ours are to those of the beasts that perish, intellects vast and cool and unsympathetic, regarded this earth with envious eyes, and slowly and surely drew their plans against us.

Stapledon, who acknowledged Wells' influence on him as like "his debt to the air he breathes" (letter to Wells, 16 Oct 1931), also used this confrontation of scales:

> But elsewhere in the solar system life of a very different kind was seeking, in its own strange manner, ends incomprehensible to man, yet at bottom identical with his own ends. And presently the two were to come together, not in co-operation (*Last and First Men,* chapter 7, part 3).

14

Clarke too uses confrontation of scales, from his earliest mature writing (*AFN*) set a billion years in the future to his latest:

> Could there be beasts among the stars, to whom men would be as insignificant as the lice upon the whale? (*IE*, chapter 40).

Yet Clarke is not merely reproducing the techniques of his predecessors. In the movement from early Wells to Clarke, we find an increasing optimism and spiritualistic acceptance of humanity's minor place in the cosmos. In *The Time Machine* (1895), which Clarke regards as Wells' masterpiece (Bernstein, p. 62), the reader sees the degeneration of *Homo sapiens* into the ruthless Morlocks and the effete Eloi of 802,701 A.D. and, briefly, sees the Earth utterly bereft of our heirs in the year 40,000,000. The tale is cautionary, and to that extent hopeful, but it is not the less bleak for that. True, the narrator retains Weena's gift to the Time Traveller—

> two strange white flowers . . . to witness that even when mind and strength had gone, gratitude and a mutual tenderness still lived on in the heart of man (Epilogue).

—but the Time Traveller himself does not live out his second trip to the future in order to return. Our futures may be slipping through our fingers.

Stapledon believes that we are doomed. In *Last and First Men* the human race metamorphoses through eighteen radically different stages still recognizably human, if not in shape, then in spirit. But eventually even humankind itself must metamorphose and leave nothing behind it. Unlike Wells, who in *The Time Machine* sees humanity as *the* spirit in the universe, Stapledon sees humanity as only one manifestation of the spiritual, and a special manifestation at that. Hence, despite mankind's extinction in his novel, *Last and First Men* ends with a warm and nostalgic self-satisfaction:

> Great are the stars, and man is of no account to them. But man is a fair spirit, whom a star conceived and a star kills. He is greater than those bright blind companies. For though in them there is incalculable potentiality, in him there is achievement, small, but actual . . . Man himself in his degree is eternally a beauty in the eternal form of things. It is very good to have been man . . . For we shall make after all a fair conclusion to this brief music that is man.

This nostalgia is the dominant tone of John W. Campbell's "Twilight." First published in the November 1934 *Astounding Stories,* under the pseudonym Don A. Stuart, this short story, which Clarke claims had a strong impact on his own writing (*LC*, Introduction), tells of a far future long

15

after machines have been perfected and when for that very reason humanity has begun to degenerate:

> The machines that couldn't stop, because they had been started, and the little men had forgotten how to stop them, or even what they were for, looking at them and listening—and wondering.

The crucial evolutionary change has been the demise of the urge to do science: "Man had lost the instinct of curiosity." Wells and Stapledon see the final end of things, but Campbell, with his faith in science, does not. His solution is ever more change:

> When the builders made those cities, they forgot one thing. They didn't realize that things shouldn't go on forever.

Clarke, like Wells and Stapledon, uses the confrontation of scales to put human activities in perspective. In *2001*, for example, Astronaut David Bowman, racing toward the outer reaches of the solar system, happens to be thinking of Earthly national rivalries when he glances at the scene behind him:

> From his present viewpoint, looking back on Earth as a dim star almost lost in the Sun, such considerations now seemed ludicrously parochial (chapter 31).

However, not even Bowman's change into the Star-Child at the end of *2001* signals the end of the human race, for that new entity comes back to Earth to contemplate it, and finally, we trust, to help it transcend itself. The faith in change that comes with modern science, faith like Campbell's, becomes in the writings of Arthur C. Clarke a fully accepted optimism that represents a development from the earlier speculation of Wells and Stapledon, an optimism to which many readers obviously respond enthusiastically.

The first important writer to combine the confrontation of scales with a faith in progressive science was not a fiction writer at all but the distinguished scientist J. D. Bernal whom Clarke refers to as an "Olympian entity" (*GP*, chapter 5) and to whom Stapledon acknowledges his own debt in the Preface to *Star Maker* (1937). In his very first book, a scientific extrapolation into possible futures called *The World, the Flesh and the Devil* (1929), Bernal not only postulates spherical space stations but immediately jumps from their possibility to their mode of existence: "the essential positive activity of the globe or colony would be in the development, growth and reproduction of the globe" (chapter 2). This growth-for-its-

16

own-sake attitude characterizes a certain kind of whole-hearted acceptance of the change science may work. Bernal embraced this attitude:

> The progress of the future depends no longer on physiological evo-lution but on the reaction of intelligence on a material universe (chapter 4).

In Bernal's agile mind, these reactions were not mere inventions but the dizzying confrontations of scale we have seen in the fiction writers:

> Finally, consciousness itself may end or vanish in a humanity that has become completely etherialized, losing the close-knit organism, becoming masses of atoms in space communicating by radiation, and ultimately perhaps resolving itself entirely into light. That may be an end or a beginning, but from here it is out of sight (chapter 3).

Bernal's brand of imaginative onrush flavors Clarke's own transcendent climaxes of humanity metamorphosed into a group mind *(CE)* or mind it-self metamorphosing into the very powers of evil and goodness *(CS)*. What-ever may be beyond, however, for Clarke as for Bernal, the end is no end but only a furthest point of today's imagining, and Clarke's mind, like that of so many scientists, tries always to imagine further tomorrow.

Clarke pays his homage to the scientific dreamers. Like Percival Lowell, the aristocratic astronomer who wrote such books as *Mars as the Abode of Life* (1908), Clarke wants to believe in the habitability of the planets. He never has humanity confined to Earth by nature alone and indeed at least indicates extraterrestrial habitation in most of his novels *(SM, IS, EL, CS, DR, FM, DI, 2001, RWR, IE* and *FOP*. Most of these works refer to a Martian city known as Port Lowell. In *2001* Clarke even ponders on the adequacy of Saturn "as an abode of life" (chapter 32). In *Glide Path* (chapter 8) Clarke attributes radar—which figures in his mind as perhaps the most significant invention of our age—to Hugo Gernsback. This inven-tor/editor published his own serial novel, *Ralph 124C41+: A Romance of the Year 2660,* in his own magazine, *Modern Electrics,* in 1911. The novel is creaky but remembered for two reasons. First, it was produced by the man who founded *Amazing Stories,* the first science fiction magazine and for whom a prestigious annual science fiction award, the Hugo, is named; second, it comprises a veritable catalogue of the inventions that the twen-tieth century was to perfect, often complete with technical details and diagrams. When Clarke in his fiction is not spinning out his optimistic and transcendental visions, he is, like Lowell or Gernsback, engrossing his reader with scientific detail.

Sometimes scientific details are offered in Clarke's fictions merely as entertaining throwaways, bits of arcana from his well-filled storeroom of intellectual oddments. In *The Sands of Mars,* for example, we read that

> on Mars . . . water under normal pressure boiled at around sixty degrees Centigrade, and cooks who forgot this elementary fact usually met with disaster (chapter 12).

Three years later in *Earthlight* we read that

> One of the minor discomforts of life on the Moon is that really hot drinks are an impossibility—water boils at about seventy degrees centigrade in the oxygen-rich, low-pressure atmosphere universally employed (chapter 7).

In neither of these novels are the implications of the Kinetic Theory of Gases very much more than decoration, though admittedly a sort of decoration that implicitly suggests the wisdom of knowing science and thinking scientifically. But in some works, the exploration in human terms of scientific detail becomes our major interest.

A Fall of Moondust may well be in part inspired by Campbell's *The Moon Is Hell* (1950), a highly detailed study of a group struggling to survive until their rescue from a lunar gypsum mine. In Clarke's novel, a tourist bus, in form "a grounded spaceship" (chapter 1), is used to provide Moon tours across a wide sea of dust, a dust produced in the lunar vacuum by eons of meteroite bombardment, dust so frictionless and fine that it flows like a liquid. The bus pushes across the surface of this sea like a boat by using huge rubber propellers. Due to a freak seismic event, the bus gets swallowed in the sea. What to do? The wealth of detail involved in the catastrophe and its solution is extraordinary. For example, long before anyone realizes what precisely has gone wrong, the bus captain recognizes that his vehicle had been designed to contain pressure, not withstand pressure like that exerted by the dust now above him. To help relieve the hull, he wordlessly increases the air pressure a notch while the stewardess passes out refreshments.

> . . . they heard a very English voice call out: "I say, Miss—this is the first decent cup of tea I've drunk on the Moon. I thought no one could make it here. My congratulations."
> . . . That was true enough; now that he had put up the cabin pressure, water must be boiling at nearly its normal, sea-level temperature back on Earth (chapter 4).

In this novel the matter of boiling point is not a throwaway. The increase

18

in pressure is an emergency expedient that occurs to someone who knows the scientific facts and theories; the possible panic of the passengers is to some extent dependent on no one noticing why that tea tastes good and inferring from it the danger the captain fears. The whole novel revolves around such matters of science and our reactions to it. The reader's own rush to design a rescue procedure for the sunken vehicle echoes the frantic rescue efforts of the characters both within the tourbus and back at the base. Here is a work that ignores vision for the sake of pure scientific thinking and humanizes that thinking so that it can challenge and entertain us. *A Fall of Moondust* is the best example of a faith in science that runs throughout Clarke's fictions, no matter how much other individual works may concern such apparent tragedies as the passing of humanity.

Given Clarke's love of science, one must point to his technical education as a major influence on his fiction. He was from boyhood gifted in mathematics and science and, not having much spare money, he learned an intimate respect for technology by crafting his own scientific instruments, including telescopes. His years at the Exchequer made him adept at computation. The single short story "Jupiter Five" required "twenty or thirty pages of orbital calculations" *(RFT,* Preface) to insure that everything reported in the narrative was true to classical mechanics. (Of course, his very facility sometimes made Clarke too casual. For example, in "Summertime on Icarus," *[TTW]* we find "a world only two miles in diameter" such that "fifteen square miles of jagged nickle-iron covered most of the asteroid's surface." Assuming a spherical body, one for which the word "diameter" would be apt, the surface area should be πd^2 or about 12.6 square miles.) Clarke's technical education continued during World War II when he went to the Royal Air Force electronics school, trained on radar, and eventually became a radar instructor. He acted as the Technical Officer on the experimental trials of the first Ground Controlled Approach radar (" 'There's only one thing bigger than radar, and you know what *that* is' "--the atomic bomb. *[GP,* chapter 14]), an experience that gave him first-hand acquaintance with working scientists and the crucial social importance of new technology. This activity was clearly central in preparing his mind for what Clarke has modestly called "the only original idea of my life" in "I Remember Babylon" *(TTW)*, geostationary communications satellites, the basis of so much of modern life. He first publsihed this idea in a technical journal, but his particular concern for comsats grew into a general exploration of the impact of technology on human communication, Clarke's most pervasive theme. The G.C.A. experience led directly to his most autobiographical novel, *Glide Path*, but held more important and deeper meanings for him as well.

He mustered out of the RAF as a Flight Lieutenant and on the basis of his wartime performance was able to attend King's College, London on a grant. In a very short time which reflected both his abilities and his prior military education, he graduated with First Class Honours in physics and mathematics. On the strength of that, he secured a job as Assistant Editor for *Science Abstracts.* For the better part of two years, he supervised and participated in digesting the mountain of scientific papers that had accumulated during the war but had been forbidden publication by wartime security regulations. As he stocked his mind with the very newest scientific ideas, Clarke continued his writing and, when his income as a writer exceeded that as an editor, he left his post with the journal.

In 1950 he met Mike Wilson, a then teenage science fiction fan who also loved skindiving. Wilson introduced Clarke to this sport and the two soon formed a partnership for exploration. Clarke now lives in Sri Lanka in large part, he claims, because of its magnificent coastal reefs. This explorative interest led directly to much of Clarke's non-fiction, to *The Deep Range* and *Dolphin Island,* and more generally to a habitual analogy in Clarke's fiction between sea and space, an analogy made obvious in the lunar sea of dust *(FM),* the Odyssey parallel in *2001,* the snorkeling episodes in *Imperial Earth,* the frequent reverence for free water (like that Alvin shows when he leaves his sealed city in both *Against the Fall of Night* and *The City and the Stars*), and in such titles as *Islands in the Sky; Across the Sea of Stars; From the Ocean, From the Stars;* and *The Fountains of Paradise.*

One final biographical detail may well be important to understanding the fiction of Arthur C. Clarke. He was born into a close family which has remained close despite the years and miles, but a family that felt the "effective absence" (letter to me of 28 April '79) of the father. Arthur was "brought up in my aunt's and grandmother's household" (letter) while his mother ran the farm purchased by his father after the war (Bernstein, p. 44). Charles Clarke died when Arthur was in his early teens and this removed the possibility of Arthur's coming to know his father as an adult. These personal facts, of course, are not inevitably important in determining Clarke's career as a writer, but one cannot help noticing that there are no strong father-son relationships in Clarke's fiction. In revising *Against the Fall of Night* to produce *The City and the Stars,* he changed Alvin's mode of creation so that his initially inconsequential parents became inconsequential *foster*-parents. In *The Sands of Mars* the middle-aged main character meets and befriends a young man whom he discovers to be his son; but since the younger man has already come to terms with his own past, the older man believes it kinder to conceal his paternity, which he does. In *Islands in the Sky* sixteen-year-old Roy Malcolm has stick-in-the-mud parents but is encouraged to visit the orbital satellites by his unmarried Uncle Jim. In *Childhood's End,* the only case of a loving father-son relationship, the relationship breaks apart when Jeffrey Greggson is transformed into a part of the psychic overmind and leaves his father George stranded on Earth. In *2001*, it is when Frank Poole's parents come on the viewscreen to wish him a happy birthday that the computer Hal contrives to first manifest the malfunction that will lead to Poole's death. In *Imperial Earth* the three generations of Makenzies are not in fact fathers and sons but identical twins cloned from each other at about thirty-five year intervals. In *The Fountains of Paradise*, Vannevar Morgan's nephew appears just in time to make the hero newly regret his own childlessness for a moment—just before his death. Clarke, at least according to the standard biographical sources, has remained unmarried since his divorce and has no children.

A total absence of strong father-son relationships would be very odd indeed considering the world in general and science fiction in particular. The immensely popular work of Robert A. Heinlein shows how important that relationship can be. Clarke does sometimes show us relationships between older men and learning younger men or adolescents. Excluding the odd case of the Makenzies *(IE)*, these relationships are almost always between a youngster and an established scientist/administrator who never has any children, and rarely a mate, on the scene. This is apparent in Jesserac's tutelage of Alvin in the second version of the Diaspar story *(CS)*, obvious in Professor Kazan's virtual adoption of Johnny Clinton in the juvenile novel *Dolphin Island*, and perhaps most pointed in Professor Schuster's image in the mind of Alan Bishop *(GP)*. This semi-autobio-. graphical character undergoes his reluctant sexual initiation and accepts responsibility only in the Professor's absence. After initiation and after acceptance, Alan becomes a fully functional and clearly admirable officer. In the case of this man who has helped shape two generations of writers, those acts form a body of writing that thrills at first encounter and then rewards our most careful attention.

It takes a lifetime to make a writer. Whatever the quirks of reading and experience, the chance encounters with earlier writers or deepsea divers or war or death, it takes something else to make an artist: a talent perhaps, a genius, something called imagination. In expressing his passionate love of the details of science and his sometimes overpowering spiritual vision, whether treating these separately or together, Arthur C. Clarke is an artist. To the extent that we can ever know others, it must be through their acts. In the case of this man who has helped shape two generations of writers, those acts form a body of writing that thrills at first encounter and then rewards our most careful attention.

21

CHILDHOOD'S END

The first of Clarke's major works to win wide public acclaim, *Childhood's End* is really two novels in one. The bulk of the work concerns the evolution of utopias from a peace imposed upon humanity to humanity's own self-organization for aesthetic and material well being. The smaller part of the work, but the more memorable, is the interwoven story of *Homo sapiens'* near-brush with extinction into death and its final extinction through transcendence into something utterly different, something—we presume—higher. Members of that future, transformed race are linked mind to mind in a single incomprehensibly powerful entity which is naturally both energetic and stable in ways no mere utopia could ever be. Now we may be children, but our children evolve into creatures, or a creature, divorced from humanity and more godlike. In this apotheosis, by which the evolutions of utopia and of the human race converge, we find *Childhood's End*.

The novel opens with a Prologue (set sometime in the late 1970s) in which we see the activities of scientists about to launch the first ship into space, the first full-scale attempt to harness the new "atomic drive." At just that critical moment, monstrous flying saucers are seen above the world's cities. Space flight has been achieved, but not by the people of Earth. The focal scientist "felt no regrets as the work of a lifetime was swept away . . . . The human race was no longer alone."

In the first part of the novel, "Earth and the Overlords," the aliens establish themselves in Earth's skies, and their spokesman Karellen issues his very few directives through the good offices of the Secretary General of the United Nations, Rikki Stormgren.

> "You may kill one another if you wish . . . and that is a matter between you and your own laws. But if you slay, except for food or in self-defense, the beasts that share your world with you—then you may be answerable to me" (chapter 3).

In addition to this general demonstration of their reverence for life, the Overlords apply a single constraint: "The stars are not for Man." Although the scientist of the Prologue had no regrets at losing a lifetime of work and although most people are shown to be so demoralized by the obvious fact of the Overlord's technical accomplishments that they abandon creative science, still there might be some individuals who would rebel. These must be stopped. As Karellen explains years later,

When we arrived, you were on the point of destroying yourselves with the powers that science had rashly given you. Without our intervention, the Earth today would be a radioactive wilderness (chapter 14).

Why, one may ask, should these superior creatures be concerned to save humanity? The first implicit answer is merely that *Homo sapiens* is worth it, that humanity is, despite the existence of the Overlords and their superior science, the spiritual center of the universe. But, of course, Clarke would not indulge in such simplistic homocentrism, such indulgent human egocentrism. These Overlords are not gods from the flying machine. In a later novel he even ridicules "the flying saucer religion [that once] flourished among the lunatic fringe of mankind" *(FM,* chapter 27). We ultimately learn that the Overlords have their ulterior motive. Human beings can evolve into something transcendent but the Overlords cannot. "We represent the ends of two different evolutions . . . . Our potentialities are exhausted, but yours are still untapped" (chapter 20). The Overlords want to be "midwives," to help the human race toward that giant step of evolution—which the Overlords call "Total Breakthrough"—so that they can study the process and perhaps learn how to correct their own fated failing. How do they know that *Homo sapiens* is nearly ready? They have been told so in some unspecified way by the "Overmind" whose instrument they are.

> . . . the road to the stars was a road that forked in two directions
> . . . . At the end of one path were the Overlords . . . . And at the end
> of the other path . . . lay the Overmind, whatever it might be, bearing the same relation to man as man bore to amoeba (chapter 23).

Here in a typical confrontation of scales, we recognize the God of the book and see that God has sent the Overlords, his guardian angels, to Earth to help mankind toward grace. This is not a simplistic homocentrism at all, but it is homocentrism indeed.

Dwelling on the protection of the Overlords, the first part of the novel chronicles the slow acceptance of the inevitable decline of nationalism and organized religion. Nationalism in Clarke's writing always dissolves when seen from a cosmic perspective. Stormgren, arguing that the unification of Earth under the Overlords represents a logical extension of such consolidations as the creation of the Common Market, remarks that

> "To the Overlords . . . the Earth probably is a great deal smaller
> than Europe seemed to our fathers—and their outlook, I submit, is
> more mature than ours" (chapter 2).

23

Religion fails because the Overlords present humanity with a machine that allows direct observation of the past, thus allowing people to "know all that is false in the stories they believe" (chapter 2). These developments do not come without resistance. Stormgren is kidnapped by extremists at one point, and the Spaniards try to defy the Overlords by continuing bull-fighting at another. But Stormgren is easily rescued and one jolt of searing but harmless pain delivered to ten thousand *aficionados* makes cruelty to animals seem suddenly unappealing. The strongest dramatic interest in this section comes from the unwillingness of the Overlords to reveal themselves. There is endless speculation among those chafing under the mild yoke that these aliens may seem beneficent but clearly have something to hide.

Fifty years later, in "The Golden Age," the Overlords reveal themselves to the generation that has grown up under their care. The Overlords fulfill precisely the historical image of devils, right down to the stubby horns and the leathery wings. How such a physical coincidence could occur is at first left a mystery, but we do learn that they hid themselves so that their serv-ice to mankind would not be rejected on superficial grounds. Most of this section of the novel contains a tour of the world functioning now as a tech-nological utopia, everyone working only if he wishes and at what he wishes, no one lacking for material goods, transport, medicine. The details of this state of affairs, like the details of the lunar rescue in *A Fall of Moondust*, are engrossing in their own right, but they do not alone sustain the novel. First, there is "the supreme enemy of all Utopias—boredom" (chapter 6). And second, there are the continuing questions about the Overlords, their real motives and their extraordinary appearance.

In this section we read of a party at the home of Rupert Boyce, a man who owns a famous collection of occult books. This library "presumably . . was simply Rupert's particular form of escapism" (chapter 7). "Escap-ism" means here, surely, something frivolous. The human guests are de-lighted to find that one of the rare but honored Overlords is himself a guest in the Boyce home. Rashaverak is a bit late coming downstairs for the party because "Rupert's library is a difficult place from which to es-cape." This second use of the word "escape" is quite different from the first for the Overlords are everywhere acknowledged for their intellectual superiority. While the occult seems an escape from the real world to us, the real world represents an escape from the occult to the Overlords. By repeating the word "escape" in two contexts on a single page, Clarke sug-gests that there may be a deeper reality than that which we see in "the real world." In addition, by potentially validating "escape," Clarke validates the reading of such "escape literature" as science fiction, including *Childhood's End*. Pointed repetition of this variety doubles a word or image in

the text to imbue it with new richness. The technique of doubling for richness, which is here applied to the notion of escape, is used throughout
Clarke's writings. In particular, he uses the technique in this book to make
us reconsider our notions of the devil. The full force of this technique is
often clear only on a second reading, as when we come across a line like
this about Karellen's hiding: " 'Why the devil won't he show himself?' "
(chapter 2).

Although Rashaverak shows himself at the Boyce party, he does not
participate. A séance is held and when one of the characters asks the ouija
board where the Overlords come from the answer is "NGS 549672" (chapter 8). Jean Morrell collapses in her seat, a guest named Jan Rodricks
snatches the paper on which the answer is written, and Rashaverak says
nothing. Most of the guests are primarily disturbed by Jean's apparent ill-
ness, but we readers feel that séances are perhaps something more than
mere diversions for the bored denizens of utopia.

In "The Last Generation" we see Jean now married to George Greggson,
her date at Boyce's. Although they have whatever they want, including
young Jeffrey and their infant daughter Jennifer, they are still vaguely un-
easy. They investigate New Athens, an ideal community set up on an
island according to the plan of a Jew named Ben Salomon who never lived
to see the fulfillment of his dream. This Moses figure reminds us of the
House of Salomon that ruled the scientific utopia of *New Atlantis* (1627)
imagined by Francis Bacon. New Athens is not a centralized technological
utopia but a democratic one, "what the old Athens might have been had it
possessed machines instead of slaves, science instead of superstition"
(chapter 15). But this most ideal of ideal states, in which each member
strives to do *"something . . .* better than anyone else" (chapter 17), is
merely the last in a long line of failures. It exists, of course, only because
the Overlords have supplied mankind with technology and have made war
ridiculous. New Athens cannot progress because these same Overlords, by
their mere presence and by their prohibition of space travel, have knocked
the stuffing out of scientific curiosity. The very best of mankind are now
virtuoso performers, but never creators.

Some, however, refuse to accept such a situation. Jan Rodricks has discovered that "NGS 549672" is the identification number of a star in an
astronomical catalogue, a star forty light-years from Earth. He gambles
that this is the home of the Overlords and contrives to stow away on their
ship by making himself a cabin in a life-size diorama of a whale and giant
squid fighting that is being sent to the Overlords' planet. Since their ship
travels at nearly the speed of light, Jan will age less than two months on
the voyage while Earth passes through forty years. He succeeds in reaching
the system the Overlords call Carina, probably with Karellen's acquies-

cence. We get a tour of the Overlord's home world and then the narrative returns to Earth and the startling transformations the Overlords have been awaiting.

The Greggson children have begun to change. Slowly but surely they develop premonitory powers; then telepathic powers; and finally telekinetic powers. They go into worldwide communion with other children like themselves as "Total Breakthrough" spreads like an "epidemic" (chapter 19) through all the human population under the age of ten. Finally these children, as radically separated from their fathers as any in Clarke's fiction, join in silent communion as they float off naked and self-sufficient into the darks of space. Jan Rodricks, who has returned after eighty Earth years but aged only four of his relativistic months, sees the end of our species as the departing children obliterate the world with their mental powers. They are no longer of the world; they are going into the heavens to join the Overmind. This is the ultimate utopia that we can imagine, the descent of grace in the form of an evolutionary leap.

Such a leap recalls the fiction of Olaf Stapledon. In *Odd John* (1935) he tells the story of a man in whom a rare gene for psychic powers has bred true. John slowly contacts others like himself, and finally they set up a colony on an island so as to avoid the envy of ordinary humans. But ordinary people will not leave these extraordinary ones alone, for, as John explains, " '*Homo sapiens* reached his limit a million years ago' " and John seems dangerous because he is not of our race:

> "If the species as whole, or a large proportion of the world population, were to be divinely inspired, so that their nature became truly human at a stride, all would soon be well . . . . At one time . . . I thought I should simply take charge of the world and help *Homo sapiens* to remake himself on a more human plan. But now I realize that only what men call 'God' could do that. Unless perhaps a great invasion of superior beings from another planet, or another dimension, could do it" (chapter 10).

Here in a single paragraph of Stapledon is the suggestion for so much of what we see developed in *Childhood's End*. But while Stapledon the philosopher gives a reasonable genetic basis for his community, the rarity of the gene and the slow ingathering of people born with it, Clarke-the-scientist flies in the face of modern biology. And he does this for a reason.

Modern genetics tells us that mutations occur only in sex cells, usually by stray radiation or by some breakdown in the mechanism by which the haploid chromosomal package is produced or recombined to form the diploid zygote, the fertilized seed that will become the new individual. After this moment of conception, no mutation can occur; no physical rearrangement of the non-sex cells of an individual will be reproduced in its offspring; successful mutations spread by successive reproduction. Stapledon understood these facts and used them. Clarke may have understood these facts but he discarded them. The "mutation" that finally hits humankind's "evolutionary line" in *Childhood's End* strikes children in inverse proportion to their age for the younger children "had so much less to unlearn" (chapter 18). Despite the wealth of technical detail in this book and in Clarke's work generally, here he utterly ignores modern science.

It is just barely conceivable, despite his obvious scientific erudition, that Clarke does not understand mutations. In *Imperial Earth* Malcolm Makenzie cannot have normal children because "a stray photon that had been cruising through space since the cosmic dawn had blasted his hopes for the future" (chapter 2). Instead of normal reproduction, Malcolm has an offspring cloned, that is, grown from one of his non-sex cells. (Cloning is already in commercial use by breeders of rare flowers and has been used successfully on laboratory animals as complex as frogs.) Since the genetic instructions for producing the sex cells are, by definition, undamaged in the normal non-sex cell, Colin the clone should be able to reproduce. But, perhaps here to avoid fathers and sons, Clarke asserts that "being Malcolm's duplicate, he too carried in his loins the fatal Makenzie gene" (chapter 8). Colin, in turn, somehow passes this defect on to his clone, our hero Duncan. Clarke appends an "Additional Note" to the novel in which he acknowledges that "expert readers" have spotted this fundamental error and says he understands but hopes some geneticist will figure a way out for him:

> Meanwhile, for those who refuse to be placated, I can only fall back upon what is known in the trade as Bradbury's Defense . . . "So I hit him."

In other words, Clarke, who can write whole novels that compel by their scientific detail alone, *refuses* to accept the accepted beliefs of science. Why?

In *Childhood's End*, with Rikki acting Moses to Karellen's God and Ben Salomon acting Moses to the people of New Athens, with Jan Rodricks supplying the role of Jonah and an infinite and incomprehensible Overmind sending his ministering devils to aid humanity, we find ourselves subtly embroiled in a tale with profound Biblical resonances. Total Breakthrough is not, as in *Odd John*, the result of mutation; it is the descent of Grace. When Grace does descend, or when a work of literature makes us believe it can descend, we have our deepest yearnings for human importance satisfied. James Blish has suggested that *Childhood's End* is so satis-

27

fying a work because we have all had the childish power fantasy of coming back in a rocket ship to lord it over those like our parents who once thwarted us (William Atheling, Jr., *More Issues At Hand*, chapter 3). This may be part of our response, of course, but personally I do not identify myself with the Overlords but with the poignant loss the parents experience, one I've seen all parents undergo as their children's childhoods ended, and with the children who gain power beyond the comprehension of their parents. In this case that gain comes not as the reward of individual worth but as the gift to the race of a cosmic consciousness that looks upon humankind with benevolence. Mythically the message of this novel is not one of science destroying religion but of religion consoling humanity in the vastness of space. *Childhood's End* throws science out to make that much more vivid its homocentric map of the spiritual universe.

Clarke's homocentrism, applied not only to space but to time, repudiates the normal Aristotelian sense of temporal cause and effect. We are told that at the séance the star catalogue number could not have been picked out of Rashaverak's mind because he was unacquainted with human astronomical nomenclature. Instead, the number came from Jeffrey Greggson, at that time "a mind not yet born." Rashaverak explains that "Time is very much stranger than you think" (chapter 18). Once the Overlords reveal themselves, people assume that they had visited the Earth in mankind's racial past, botched a job of helping those ancient Earthmen, and hence humanity has retained a racial memory of the Overlords' form which is associated with evil. But Rashaverak explains otherwise:

> "There was only one event that could have made such an impact upon humanity. And that event was not at the dawn of history, *but at its very end* . . . that memory was not of the past, but of the *future*—of those closing years when your race knew that everything was finished . . . And because we were there, we became identified with your race's death" (chapter 23).

In *Imperial Earth*, also, though it is not a visionary novel, Clarke explains that Duncan Makenzie

> caught a momentary glimpse in the Mirror of Time, reflecting something that had not yet occurred—and something that must be awesomely important for it to have succeeded in reversing the flow of causality (chapter 42).

Clarke sounds here not like a man with an allegiance to modern physics and mathematics but to the sort of archetypal coincidence Jung calls "synchronicity," which means all time existing at once. Clarke even admiringly cites Arthur Koestler's Jungian treatise, *The Roots of Coincidence* (1972), in a note to *Imperial Earth*. In God's eye, all things happen at once. The Old Testament prefigures the New, and in the eternity of myth, the flow of history becomes insignificant.

Arthur C. Clarke's vision makes little allowance for the normal passage of values from parent to child, but he yearns nonetheless, as so many of us do, for a secure sense of parentage in the world. One would give up much to validate our fantasies not of power only but of homocentrism. Jan Rodricks was aching to know where the Overlords came from when he attended the séance. For a moment, after Jean collapsed, he doubted what had just happened:

> It was an impossible coincidence. NGS 549672 *must* be the home of the Overlords. Yet to accept the fact violated all Jan's cherished ideas of scientific method. Very well—let them be violated (chapter 9).

Clarke rewards Jan's leap of faith with his longed-for trip to the stars. In *Childhood's End* he rewards his readers' leap of faith with a vision of all humanity's transcendent evolution toward a union with an Overmind that loves us. No wonder so many readers feel this novel, though flawed in its science, to be perfect in its spirit.

THE CITY AND THE STARS

Like a glowing jewel, the city lay upon the breast of the desert. Once it had known change and alteration, but now Time passed it by. Night and day fled across the desert's face, but in the streets of Diaspar it was always afternoon, and darkness never came. The long winter nights might dust the desert with frost, as the last moisture left in the thin air of Earth congealed—but the city knew neither heat nor cold. It had no contact with the outer world; it was a universe itself.

The city of Diaspar, like the castle of "Sleeping Beauty," hovers in the near dead "always afternoon." A world sealed off from the wider world, the city awaits renewed contact. Just as the enchanted castle existed "long, long ago," Diaspar exists in that far future when the very atmosphere of Earth has thinned. Thus begins a fairy tale vision that haunted Clarke for at least twenty years. In 1935 a scene flashed into his mind, a scene which he wrote down and saved. Two years later he returned to that scene and began the first draft of a novel. In 1946, after writing five full versions of the story, Clarke thought he had finished (*LC,* Introduction). He published his work in the November 1948 *Startling Stories* as *Against the Fall of Night.* Although this was printed separately as a book in 1953, Clarke was still unable to resist the call of the tale. He rewrote it again, nearly doubled its size, and in 1956 published one of his greatest works, *The City and the Stars.*

This novel, like so many fairy tales, follows the adventures of a young man who wants to make his own way in the unknown outer world. Alvin is born into a fairy tale landscape. Diaspar—the name itself seems magical—overflows with such wonders as the Tower of Loranne, hypnone projectors that transfer knowledge right into one's mind, and machines, myriad machines, that respond instantly to human thought. Alvin conceives of a couch and it materializes before him; he wishes to see a friend and so finds himself projected visually into his company; he desires some delectable food and it emerges from the synthesizer. No witch ever granted more wishes. In the mythology of this work, the "Invaders" were driven back from Earth at the ancient "Battle of Shalmirane." When Alvin does finally get outside Diaspar, with the help of a "Jester" named Khedron and a magical transport system left over from "the Dawn Ages," he discovers a pastoral world named Lys with telepathic inhabitants, some talking animals (chapter 11) and a creature who hints to him of the mysteries of the "Seven Suns" (chapter 19).

This work is so much a fairy tale that one may think it is not science fiction, but it is that as well. The worlds of Lys and Diaspar represent the stable endproducts of two divergent lines of human evolution. Benjamin Disraeli had seen in *Sybil, or the Two Nations* (1845) that people occupying different social roles, workers and managers for example, might someday be radically opposed. In *The Time Machine* (1895) H. G. Wells projected that notion eight hundred thousand years into the future where his Time Traveller comes to recognize "that Man had not remained one species, but had differentiated into two distinct animals" (chapter 5), the Morlocks and the Eloi, both of which are defective by our current standards. The reason for the devolution of the human race into pampered, delicate and ineffectually moronic Eloi is particularly telling:

> What, unless biological science is a mass of errors, is the cause of human intelligence and vigour? Hardship and freedom: conditions under which the active, strong, and subtle survive and the weaker go to the wall (chapter 4).

Pastoral Lys is peopled with kindhearted telepaths, morally admirable individuals much finer than the Eloi, to be sure. But they use their powers to preserve a stagnant culture, one based, like the utopia of William Morris' *News From Nowhere* (1890), on individual free choice of activity and an inherited technology that performs the unchosen tasks: " 'All work which would be irksome to do by hand is done by immensely improved machinery.' " (Morris, ch. 15) Just as Wells' dark novel is a call for social interaction to avoid catastrophe, so Clarke's optimistic novel is a call for social interaction to avoid wasting the potentialities of our race.

The differences between Diaspar and Lys are fundamental. While the people of the villages of Lys are telepaths, pastoralists, and psychological geniuses, the people of sealed Diaspar are cowering xenophobes who happen to be immortal. Their immortality, like so much else, comes to them as a technological legacy from the past. The people and their city had been designed together. However, just as the people in Campbell's "Twilight" are pampered into weakness and decadence by their technology seven million years from now, so too the curiosity of the people living over a billion years after Diaspar's founding has all but atrophied. As it is explained to Alvin,

> our ancestors learned how to analyze and store the information that would define any specific human being—and to use that information to re-create the individual . . . At any moment, Alvin, only a hundredth of the citizens of Diaspar live (chapter 2).

while the others exist only as electrical patterns in the great Memory

31

Banks. The "Central Computer" calls them forth randomly from the "Hall of Creation," full grown but young individuals to replace those who have chosen not to live again for a while by walking back into the Hall of Creation. However, as the people of Lys explain, by way of justifying their divorce from the people of Diaspar,

> the power to extend his life indefinitely might bring contentment to the individual, but brought stagnation to the race (chapter 14).

So both Lys and Diaspar have stagnated, though their stagnations are very different indeed:

> Hilvar [of Lys] had stripped off all his clothes, and for the first time Alvin saw how much the two branches of the human race had diverged. Some of the changes were merely ones of emphasis or proportion, but others, such as the external genitals and the presence of teeth, nails, and definite body hair, were more fundamental. What puzzled him most of all, however, was the curious small hollow in the pit of Hilvar's stomach . . . . By the time that Hilvar had made the functions of the navel quite clear, he had uttered many thousands of words and drawn half a dozen diagrams (chapter 11).

Just as "Sleeping Beauty" defines its own happy ending as the reawakening of the Princess and her marriage to a Prince, so *The City and the Stars* defines its desired outcome as a release of the two peoples from sterility both mental and physical. It is Alvin's role to foster the necessary social interactions.

Unlike *Childhood's End,* which uses characters only as stand-ins for whole segments of humanity, *The City and the Stars* provides us with a strong character whom we must recognize as the hero. Alvin

> was always wanting to go outside, both in reality and in dream. Yet to everyone in Diaspar, "outside" was a nightmare that they could not face (chapter 1).

Alvin's tutor Jeserac often contemplates the primes, numbers that can be divided evenly only by themselves and one. "There was a mystery about the primes that had always fascinated Man, and they held his imagination still" (chapter 6). Alvin is such a prime, the only individual in all his closed world to emerge from the Hall of Creation without any past lives.

> Whether his uniqueness was due to accident or to an ancient design [of the builders of Diaspar], he did not know (chapter 4).

but he does know that, like every diminutive fairy tale hero from Tom

Thumb to the Gallant Tailor, he must set out on a quest to see the wider world. This childlikeness is clearly crucial to understanding Clarke's novel, for, in revising *Against the Fall of Night*, he changed the people of Diaspar from long-lived humans among whom Alvin was "the only child to be born . . . for seven thousand years" *(AFN,* chapter 5) to immortals among whom Alvin "was the first child to be born . . . for at least ten million years" (chapter 2).

Alvin's unique ambition, once he discovers Lys, is "to repair the Break" between "the two surviving branches of the human race" (chapter 16). "Only a very young person could ever have thought of . . . the plan" *(AFN,* chapter 8). Such hybridization is normally considered a genetic advantage; it is clearly desireable in *The Time Machine.* The evolutionary pay-off for social interaction, of course, must lie in the future. But in an important sense, since Mankind has stagnated, the pay-off may actually lie in the past, both in the necessary reversion to the childlike and in a cultural atavism as well.

Through machinations wonderful to behold, across magic vistas and beside miraculous creatures, Alvin manages to acquire a spaceship long buried beneath desert sands. With this ship, he travels to the center of a now abandoned Galactic civilization of which humanity had once been a part. His presence there attracts Vanamonde, a creature of pure mentality. In typically homocentric words, we read that

"the creation of pure mentalities [a transcendent evolutionary leap] was the greatest achievement of Galactic civilization; in it Man played a major and perhaps a dominant part" (chapter 24).

Vanamonde, like the group entity at the end of *Childhood's End*, possesses enormous mental power and yet is in some emotional and/or spiritual sense still a child. Unlike humanity's spontaneous successors, this artificial creation is delighted to meet the race of his makers and returns to Earth only too glad to impart the eons of memories that are stored within him but that are, because he is so young by his own standards, poorly understood. The psychologists and historians of Lys go to work with Vanamonde to unravel the wonders of the race that had built Diaspar:

The recharting of the past would take centuries, but when it was finished Man would have recovered almost all that he had lost (chapter 26).

In a cultural sense, then, the happy outcome of *The City and the Stars,* although set in the far off future, is actually a reversion to what the characters regard as "long, long ago." Clarke's novel, like most fairy tales, in-

33

dulges not only the illusion of the hero's—and reader's— central position but also panders to a deep atavistic urge that has been with humanity since the story of the Fall began to make emotional sense.

The role of fertilizing agent, the young man who breaks down boundaries between static cultures to reinvigorate the human race, is clearly an important one for Clarke. Not only in the many versions of this story but in his early novella *The Lion of Comarre* as well we see a series of motifs repeated. The hero is a young man born into a static city culture who wants to discover some alternative. The world provides a pastoral contrast, some controlled wilderness which is also static. Against the inhibitions of authority figures but with the help of a friend, the hero manages to fulfill a design of the very founders of his world, a design much more sanctified by age than the mere wishes of his living elders. When the young man succeeds, his culture recognizes the wisdom inherent in his youthful desire to explore. As the story ends, we see that curiosity is again kindled, that science is about to burgeon anew and that mankind is poised once more on the road to the stars. Like the transcendent children of *Childhood's End,* humanity is once more on the path toward heaven.

In such a fairy tale of Paradise about to be regained, the Central Computer of Diaspar is a clear image for God. This omnipotent and immortal guardian of humanity is the all-knowing intelligence that materializes goods from the Memory Banks and prevents decay by operating the "Eternity Circuits" (chapter 10). When Alvin is granted an unprecedented interview with the Central Computer, he travels to the bowels of the city, to the hall meant only for machines. "It was hard to talk to a presence who filled the whole of the space around you" (chapter 16). But Alvin succeeds in dealing with this entity because he, like children always, has faith in his own importance. From early in the novel, when Alvin was first trying to discover a way out of Lys, he believed that

> the all-but-infinite intellect of the Central Computer . . . must know what [he] was doing, and, therefore, it must approve, otherwise it would have stopped him (chapter 7).

With this faith, he proceeds and in many senses of the word, he "saves" the human race. This action offers the psychological indulgence of the fairy tale in confirming the youngster's central position, the science fictional pay-off of truly cosmic stakes being gambled and won, and the religious consolation of an incomprehensibly potent entity caring for humanity.

In the world of Arthur C. Clarke, these positive values are combined in the image of space flight. "Only a space-faring culture could truly trans-

34

cend its environment, and join others in giving a purpose to creation" *(LW,* chapter 10). In *Star Maker* (1937), Olaf Stapledon's "disembodied viewpoint" "felt in the physical presence of the cosmos the psychical presence of that which we had named the Star Maker" (chapter 8). From space not only national differences seem petty but cultural ones as well. After having discovered the lost spaceship, Alvin thinks that

> of all Man's ancient powers, this surely was the one he could least afford to lose. Alvin wished he could show the world as he saw it now to the rulers of Lys and Diaspar (chapter 19).

The ending of *Against the Fall of Night* was unchanged in revising the early novel to produce *The City and the Stars.* Indeed, the following space image so struck Clarke that he could not resist using it yet again in the story he considers his best, "Transit of Earth" *(WFS,* 1970). Alvin is in space on the novel's last page and looks down at Earth to see

> at one instant both sunrise and sunset on opposite sides of the world. The symbolism was so perfect, and so striking, that they were to remember this moment all their lives.
>
> *In this Universe the night was falling; the shadows were lengthening toward an east that would not know another dawn. But elsewhere the stars were still young and the light of morning lingered; and along the path he once had followed, Man would one day go again.*

Arthur Clarke's vision of a future as good as our past captures the aspirations of religion and lends justification to science, but most of all, it gives its readers a vision of our race made worthwhile and a fairy tale we can help to come true.

2001: A SPACE ODYSSEY

The film *2001: A Space Odyssey* electrified the public at its release in 1968. The first big budget science fiction film, Stanley Kubrick's second venture into science fiction, like his first, *Dr. Strangelove*, 1964, and his next, *A Clockwork Orange*, 1971, won both critical acclaim and box office success. In all three cases, Kubrick collaborated on the screenplays with established fiction writers and then directed and edited the film himself. Brian Aldiss, in his discussion of the fiction of Arthur C. Clarke, notes that these achievements may well qualify Kubrick the filmmaker as "the great sf writer of the age" *(Billion Year Spree*, chapter 10). Clarke too has been quite generous in assigning Kubrick credit for the novel that bears only Clarke's name:

> . . . toward the end [of the collaboration] , both novel and screen-play were being written simultaneously, with feedback in both directions . . . After a couple of years of this, I felt that when the novel finally appeared it should be "by Arthur Clarke and Stanley Kubrick: based on the screenplay by Stanley Kubrick and Arthur Clarke"— whereas the movie should have the credits reversed. This still seems the nearest approximation to the complicated truth *(LW*, chapter 4).

But the authorship of the novel has not been misassigned by the publishers. First, there are many significant differences between the film and the novel, matters of great interest in themselves that affect our understanding of the respective versions but which we cannot take the space to investigate in this reader's guide. Second, any careful reading of the novel will show that its great achievement is not only in the story itself but in the synthesizing and maturing of images and ideas that have been developing throughout Clarke's career. One can easily imagine that this polished creation was enormously helped by Clarke's constant interaction with Kubrick's fine critical intelligence, but the result is still based on Clarke's materials, Clarke's skills, and Clarke's bold imagination. The novel *2001: A Space Odyssey* is Clarke's mature amalgamation of his compelling interest in scientific detail and his spiritual commitment to a homocentric and optimistic vision. In many ways, the book may be his culminating artistic achievement.

The novel is divided into six parts which are sometimes related only by theme and sequence rather than character and plot. Each part, by jumping radically forward in time or idea, not only presents its own materials but helps add new understanding to the materials of preceding sections. This trick of adding a chapter set well after the main action to provide an enriching context for that action is common in Clarke's novels that focus our interest through the suspenseful unfolding of scientific detail *(PS, SM, EL, DR, FM, FOP)*. In the early short story "Transcience" *(OSS, 1949)*, Clarke juxtaposes three radically different sections to show mankind in the prehuman, human, and post-human stages. In *2001* he again uses that early boldness of juxtaposition and the theme of human transformation but combines it with the compelling scientific details of his novels. The six parts together tell the story of mankind from his pre-human "man-ape" stage through his post-human birth as "Star-Child." The transitions from one stage to another are induced and manipulated by extrasolar intelligences much vaster than our own. The monolith image which represents these intelligences is the one constant element in the novel and in an important sense one can say that the book is about whatever the monolith is about for mankind, a subject which will be easier to discuss once we have reviewed the precise contents of the novel's six parts.

"Primeval Night" (part 1) tells the story of a man-ape the narrator calls "Moon-Watcher." In light of Clarke's own emphasis on values associated with space and the later importance of the moon to this novel, this particular man-ape's odd habit of astronomical contemplation must be seen as a fundamental and positive human trait, even though this trait has arisen spontaneously before humankind. Alien intelligences plant a monolith near Moon-Watcher's tribe's territory, and forces from the monolith control his mind and body to give him new ideas. The tribe exists in a constant state of near starvation:

> Yet the thousands of tons of succulent meat roaming over the savanna and through the bush was not only beyond their reach; it was beyond their imagination. In the midst of plenty, they were slowly starving to death (chapter 1).

The monolith plants *ideas* in the members of the tribe; these take most successfully with Moon-Watcher. He learns to use basic tools: a stone as a hammer, an antelope jawbone as a saw, a knobbed thighbone as a club, a gazelle horn as an awl or dagger. With these weapons and with the tutelage of the monolith, the man-apes begin to change their lives. They not only eat better but have the leisure to learn to kill other man-apes to defend their territory more successfully against the encroachment of a neighboring tribe. Clarke in this section seems to accept the widely-held but controversial theories made popular by Robert Ardrey in *African Genesis* (1961): *Homo sapiens* arose from killer apes who learned to use tools to defend themselves against nature and their own kind. This instinct to kill and defend and make tools transformed their kind, and these apes finally evolved into human beings. In "Expedition to Earth" (*EE*, 1953), Clarke had shown alien astronauts coming to Earth to leave tools in the hope that the gift of technology would induce the pre-human primates to evolve intelligence. In this novel the mechanism of donation, the monolith, is much more obviously spiritual and the resulting evolution is much more explicit: "The tool-makers [the apes] had been remade by their tools" (chapter 6). A consequence of this transformation is intelligence, and intelligence leads to the most significant technology of all:

> They [Moon-Watcher's far descendants] had learned to speak, and so had won their first great victory over Time. Now the knowledge of one generation could be handed on to the next, so that each age could profit from those that had gone before (chapter 6).

These human traits established, Clarke moves immediately to the year 2001.

"TMA-1" (part 2) concerns the discovery on the Moon in Tycho Crater of a Magnetic Anomaly. Excavation at the epicenter of this oddity uncovers a great ebon monolith obviously enough referred to as TMA-1. Most of this section of the novel unfolds scientific detail as we follow the trip of Dr. Heywood Floyd, presidential science advisor, to the Moon to examine the monolith himself. In Clarke's most convincing manner, we get all the intricacies of propulsion, weightlessness and artificial gravity which he has sometimes used before without so engaging a dramatic context *(PS, IS)*. We even learn that the difficulties of voiding oneself in freefall can be solved by a rotating cylindrical washroom that creates its own minor—but sufficient—gravity (chapter 9). With Floyd at the edge of the digging site, the lunar dawn rises and suddenly all nearby hear a shriek through the radios in their spacesuits. Just as in Clarke's early short story "The Sentinel" *(EE*, 1951), mankind's tampering with the monolith has set off the alarm: the message of our attainment of space flight has been sent to the stars.

"Between Planets" (part 3) shows astronauts David Bowman and Frank Poole aboard the space craft *Discovery* on their way to Saturn. Clarke reveals such wonders as hibernation to give astronauts time to reach their destination and the ability to save on food consumption, explains in detail the intricate schedule of shipboard routine, and describes the central computer that is a conscious partner of the astronauts, Hal. This HAL 9000 (for "Heuristically programmed ALgorithmic computer") had been weakly foreshadowed by Max in Clarke's "Cosmic Casanova" *(OSS*, 1958) and by OSCAR in *Dolphin Island* (and would be palely followed by ARISTOTLE in *The Fountains of Paradise*) but Hal is infinitely more important than those mere machines. Hal talks with the astronauts, plays games with them, and finally emerges as the most interesting character in the novel. We and Hal understand that the mission is to follow the signal of TMA-1 to find its receiver and perhaps those who received the message, but the astronauts do not know this. They believe themselves on a pioneering, but standard, mission, and within this framework they carry out fascinating activities including a ballistic examination of the crust of an asteroid and a Jupiter fly-by to use the giant planet's gravity to gain velocity and make a course correction. The section ends with the description of the transmissions from a probe dropped toward Jupiter. This reveals a monstrous smoking mountain sending up regular puffs of smoke rings roiling from around the outside of its base. The same image occurs in *Childhood's End* (chapter 22) where it is hinted that the mountain might be the mysterious medium by which the Overmind communicates with the Overlords. But in neither novel is this image in fact explained and the section which so forcefully sticks to scientific detail ends with an enigma.

"Abyss" (part 4) is also set aboard *Discovery*, but now things begin to go wrong. Hal sends Frank Poole outside the ship to change a presumably defective part that is not in fact defective. Finally, using the space pod "Betty," the controls of which have been turned over to Hal by Poole, Hal crushes the astronaut. We are made to understand that Hal has gone insane because he has been created to help and foster the mission and to be honest and reliable for the astronauts, but also, in the case of this particular mission, he has been instructed not to reveal the facts about TMA-1 or the mission's true purpose. This conflict of commands might merely trouble a man, but machine intelligence cannot long withstand it. Clarke had already created an insane computer in *The City and the Stars,* but in that case the higher intelligence of the Central Computer was able to cure it *(CS,* chapter 17). Here the only solution is to have David Bowman disconnect Hal's higher faculties. Hal interprets this plan as a threat to the mission and, as allowed by his secret orders, he moves to avert that threat: he opens the ship to the vacuum of space. Bowman, however, survives by crossing without spacesuit from a space pod to an emergency closet that contains oxygen and a suit. This apparently magical feat is a perfect example of Clarke's amalgamation of his vision with his concern for scientific detail. The motif had been used by him before in *Earthlight* (chapter 19) and in "Take a Deep Breath." *(OSS,* 1957) Clarke defends himself:

> The short story "Take a Deep Breath" has been strongly criticized because of its suggestion that an unprotected man could survive in the vacuum of space. Experiments with dogs and chimpanzees (which have suffered no ill-effects after *three minutes* in vacu-

um) have now completely validated this idea *(OSS,* Bibliographical Note).

In the case of *2001,* unlike the earlier examples, the survival in vacuum is not mere survival but, coming out of the emergency closet and passing the corpses of the previously hibernating astronauts, this survival has all the impact of a rebirth. Just as a transformed Moon-Watcher kills his neighbor, so Bowman emerges from his experience to attend immediately to the dismantling of Hal.

"The Moons of Saturn" (part 5) shows Bowman exploring the system of moons he was actually sent to investigate, and once there he discovers "TMA-2," a monstrously large version of the lunar monolith. The narrator takes an Olympian view and makes clear that this is all part of a plan by intelligences infinitely higher than those of mankind.

> Those who had begun that experiment [with Moon-Watcher] . . . saw how often the first faint sparks of intelligence flickered and died in the cosmic night.
> And because, in all the galaxy, they had found nothing more precious than Mind, they encouraged its dawning everywhere. They became farmers in the fields of stars; they sowed, and sometimes they reaped.
> And sometimes, dispassionately, they had to weed (chapter 37).

This Stapledonian stoicism reminds us that Bowman's success is by no means assured. Should he find these superior beings, they might foster our evolution as they once did before but they might just as easily swat us like flies. Clarke recalls in this section his typical preference for antiscientific genetics. In the first part he had written of Moon-Watcher:

> the very atoms of his simple brain were being twisted into new patterns. If he survived, those patterns would become eternal, for his genes would pass them on to future generations (chapter 3).

Now, with Bowman, "out among the stars, evolution was driving toward new goals" (chapter 37). In that drive, Bowman approaches TMA-2, and this monolith, which the narrator calls "Star Gate," flicks open and closed (chapter 40). Bowman is no longer in our solar system.

"Through the Star Gate" (part 6) tells of Bowman's extraordinary cosmic voyage, a homocentric voyage in keeping with Clarke's habitual themes:

> . . . he must surely be under the protection of some controlling and almost omnipotent intelligence . . . If so much trouble had been taken to preserve him, there was still cause for hope (chapter 43).

The voyager crosses light-years in moments, with blazing stars flickering in and out of existence around him. Bowman journeys to a galactic Grand Central Station where thousands of monoliths exist as Star Gates presumably to far-off realms. He is somehow protected while brought to the very surface of a sun and finally deposited in a replica of an Earth hotel. He takes off his spacesuit there, showers, sleeps, and in his sleep he is transformed. Bowman dies but is reborn as Star-Child, a cosmic intelligence, a mind vaster than Vanamonde's and similarly youthful. Star-Child thinks himself to our solar system and almost instantly is there. When Moon-Watcher had first dimly understood the power of his weapons, his imagination was stirred.

> Now he was master of the world, and he was not quite sure what to do next.
> But he would think of something (chapter 5).

From the very beginning of this novel, whether as the discoveries of science or as the mental transformations induced by the monoliths, imagination has been a theme and a prime value. On the last page, Star-Child out in space contemplates Earth and reacts much like Moon-Watcher:

> Then he waited, marshaling his thoughts and brooding over his still untested powers. For though he was master of the world, he was not quite sure what to do next.
> But he would think of something (chapter 47).

And what he will imagine to do, we are sure, will help *Homo sapiens* even if, as in *Childhood's End*, *Homo sapiens* is no more.

This successful amalgamation of Clarke's concerns for science and vision depends psychologically on the creation of a single dominating image that engages both. That image is the monolith. At first glance one might well think that the monolith is a phallic symbol, an emblem for procreation, and to some extent this is so. However, the monolith in one form or another is a haunting image for Clarke, and as one follows it through many works, one begins to see that its potency is much more than procreative.

In *The Lion of Commare* people live in high-rise cities. We are given a special description of the home of the scientists:

> . . . a single white pylon began to climb out of the ocean like the sword of Excalibur rising from the lake. The city known to the world as Scientia . . . (*LC*, chapter 2).

Excalibur is a magical sword that responds only to its rightful owner and defends the magic city Camelot against barbarism; Scientia, "knowledge,"

41

defends the society of its narrative world against stagnation by fostering Dick Peyton's journey to Comarre, an invasion that hybridizes the cultures and starts humanity again on a progressive road. The pylon of knowledge, then, like the sword Excalibur, thrusts into the "Great Reservation" to plant a seed, a seed not of animal life but of knowledge.

We find another monolith in *Against the Fall of Night* on the central planet of the "Seven Suns":

> The great column of white stone was perhaps twenty times the height of a man, and was set in a circle of metal slightly raised above the level of the plain. It was featureless and of its purpose there was no hint. They might guess, but they would never know, that it had once marked the zero point of all astronomical measurements *(AFN,* chapter 15).

When that image is revised by Clarke for *The City and the Stars,* it not only gains in stature but transforms itself from an instrument of science to an artifact of the spirit:

> The great column of stone was perhaps a hundred times the height of a man, and was set in a circle of metal slightly raised above the level of the plain. It was featureless and bore no inscription. For how many thousands or millions of years, wondered Alvin, had the Master's disciples gathered here to do him honor? *(CS,* chapter 20).

In both *Against the Fall of Night* and *The City and the Stars,* we find Shalmirane,

> a giant bowl half a mile deep and three miles in diameter . . . black as the rock of a world that had never known a sun . . . and ringing the entire crater was a seamless band of metal, some hundred feet wide . . . *(AFN,* chapter 7).

This image functions implicitly with that of the column, and in the later version of the novel, the bowl and the column are associated:

> . . . a column of snow-white springing from the center of an immense marble amphitheater . . . Never before in his life, even in the desolation of Shalmirane, had he been in utter silence *(CS,* chapter 20).

Shalmirane, of course, is finally revealed as a weapon, a device for focusing monstrous energies and hurling them not against the mythical Invaders but against the actual Moon when its orbit began to decay. In our current technology, the combined image of the bowl and column is perhaps best captured by the dish antennae of radar.

Radar, of course, functions centrally in Clarke's own life. He also associates the monolith or pylon with radar in many of his fictions. In *Prelude to Space* the featureless desert of the Australian launching site is dominated by the meteorological tower (part 3, chapter 2) which serves as central landmark just as the column in *Against the Fall of Night* serves as an astronomical landmark. In "The Sentinel" the monolithic beacon shoots out its radio message of mankind's arrival. In "The Light of Darkness" *(WFS,* 1964) an African dictator climbs atop the huge central antenna of a radio telescope for the device's inauguration, and at just that moment, using a mirror he had previously set up on a mountainside, a freedom-loving astronomer shoots a laser beam from his observatory by ricochet into the dictator's eyes, blinding him and ending his power. The most emotionally gripping passage in the semi-authobiographical *Glide Path* is the description of the hero's perilous climb up a three hundred foot pylon used to suspend a radar antenna. Alan Bishop only climbs the tower because his manhood is at stake; he has been all but challenged to follow his former friend *(GP,* chapter 11).

In each of these works, the monolith image is highly important but somehow never central. It combines within it the idea of knowledge and power and communication. It is only in *2001* that the image of the monolith, which in that novel serves to communicate and guide and transport, takes on also its obvious phallic potency. By the operation of the monoliths, Star-Child is born. In this work alone, Clarke faces the image squarely, makes it central to his text, and has the courage to use it not only as an emblem of communication (note his treatment of language as technology) but as the instrument of procreation.

In his last three novels, having come to grips with the monolith, Clarke can use the image more easily again, more easily, in fact, than he ever had before. In *Rendezvous With Rama* the monolith image appears as "Big Horn," the central feature of the artificial planet's propulsion system and an image of pure power (chapter 26). In *Imperial Earth* Duncan Makenzie clambers up a radar tower to follow his rival/friend Karl Helmer. This tower is part of a massive array of radar dishes called Cyclops which is intended to search for possible messages from alien intelligences. Atop the tower

It was as if the sun had exploded . . . He heard a cry from Karl . . . [who] it was obvious, could not see at all *(IE,* chapter 37).

The blinded Karl falls to the ground and is killed. In this occurrence, Clarke has reused the blinding of the dictator but now against a friend. True, Duncan is not directly the villain, but it is his own courage in climbing the monolith that creates the situation of danger that causes his bodyguards to try to temporarily blind Karl, with such fatal results. At the end of the novel, Duncan returns to Titan. He was to have cloned himself. He is a very dark black man. When his friends open the bundle he carries in his arms, they see "the little head . . . the golden hair that would soon bring back to Titan the lost glories of the distant Sun" *(IE,* chapter 43). Those are the novel's last words; the baby cloned from the dead friend is the last effect of climbing the monolith. And finally *The Fountains of Paradise* focuses almost exclusively on the construction of a forty thousand kilometer "Space Elevator," a monolithic tower reaching beyond our atmosphere. In planning this project, the novel's lonely hero, Vannevar Morgan, had

> the feeling that he was being moved by forces beyond his understanding.
>
> Yet the sense of awe had a familiar resonance. He had experienced it before, when, as a child, he had flown his kite in Kiribilli Park, beside the granite monoliths that had once been the piers of the long demolished Sydney Harbour Bridge.
>
> Those twin mountains had dominated his boyhood, and had controlled his destiny. (chapter 7)

This novel of technological detail makes explicit the image constellation of mountain, monolith, stairway and bridge: "a stairway to heaven—a bridge to the stars" (ch. 10). At ease now with the dominating image of his life, Clarke, in the book he announced as his last, can return the image to communication and transportation—"millions . . . rode in comfort and safety to the stars" (ch. 57)—as the conquering engineer dies childless yet happy.

Clarke always has difficulty in drawing father-son relationships, yet the idea of fostering growth is dear to him, expressed perhaps most germanely in the relationship of Alan Bishop to Professor Schuster. Once Clarke finally deals with the phallic image of the monolith directly in *2001,* he is able to return this image of probing and knowledge and communication—of science, in short—to its primal context of procreation. For the author, this means that he can see the monolith without fear as pure power, as in *Rendezvous With Rama,* use it to motivate his hero to reproduce not himself but his male friend, as in *Imperial Earth,* and make it the means of humanity's transformation, as in *The Fountains of Paradise.* This psychological freedom is won by the act of struggling through the many revisions of *2001,* drawing in so much of Clarke's earlier thought and facing it squarely. Having done this, having surrendered to the power of the image of the monolith, Clarke has created a book that transforms his readers, as it transforms David Bowman, into grateful recipients of a new spiritual perspective. This justly famous work achieves a unity of science and vision that leaves us, as do Stapledon's finest novels, with a sense of cosmic insight and an emotional sweep which seems to represent—and in this case does represent—the synthesis of the thoughts of a lifetime.

RENDEZVOUS WITH RAMA

There are four major awards in the field of science fiction. Each represents a different constituency. The Hugo Award is given by the fans at the annual so-called "world" science fiction convention; the Nebula Award is given by the membership of the Science Fiction Writers of America; the John W. Campbell Award is given by a distinguished panel of critics and writers; and the Jupiter Award is given by the members of ISFHE (Instructors of Science Fiction in Higher Education). *Rendezvous With Rama* is the only work to have won them all. Like *A Fall of Moondust,* which was nominated for a Hugo Award, *Rendezvous With Rama* compels us by the intricacy and challenge of its scientific detail. Unlike *A Fall of Moondust,* but quite like *2001, Rendezvous With Rama* combines its scientific exposition with an abiding philosophic concern.

The novel recounts the entrance into our solar system of an anomalous object with strange properties of reflection and an unusual trajectory. The object is finally revealed as a cylinder with a forty kilometer axis and a ten kilometer diameter. A routine survey mission is diverted to land on the object, named Rama, and exploration begins. Rama turns out to be an artificial planet with centrifugal spin creating gravity. The book is almost entirely devoted to exploration within this product of an obviously alien and unbelievably advanced culture. A prime example of the wonder of this exploration is the gravity: zero at the axis, it increases as one goes from the axis to the inner surface. The middle of Rama is encircled within by the "Cylindrical Sea." One can look across this ring-shaped body of water in the line of the axis and see it flat, but one can also look directly overhead to see its orthogonally curved surface meeting kilometers above, held in place by the centrifugal gravity. The variable gravity and cylindrical sea are but two of the scientific wonders that we encounter with Clarke's explorers.

Since we do learn about Rama at the same time as the characters, we are in a position to match wits with them to try to understand the implications of this world before the characters do. The cylindrical sea, for example, is contained by circular walls. Clarke challenges the reader to account for Raman geography:

> But for what conceivable reason was the cliff on the southern shore five hundred meters high, instead of the fifty here? (chapter 15).

Just in case we haven't stopped to consider the solution to this problem, he reminds us that it is unsolved before he solves it. " 'Of course!' " one character shouts, " 'That explains everything! The southern cliff—*now* it makes sense!' " We may stop now and think, or read on to learn on the next page that the huge cliff is necessary if we assume that Rama is not ballistic but can accelerate by means of a propulsion system at its south end. We even get the acceleration calculated for us as two percent of Earth gravity (chapter 19).

That five hundred meter sea wall presents a challenge to the reader again, and to the ingenuity of the crew, when one man gets stranded on the far shore. "He could imagine no way in which he could lower himself down the face of that half-kilometer cliff" (chapter 30). We could not be more clearly invited to imagine a solution ourselves. And a solution there is, though it would diminish the suspense of the book to reveal it here.

Not only does Clarke challenge us with his detailed creation of Rama, but he teaches us the basic science necessary to respond to those challenges. Quite early in the novel, as the crew begins to descend one of three spiral staircases dropping from the center of the northern cap to the great plain on the cylinder's inner surface, Clarke explains the nature of Coriolis forces, forces generated within Rama by its rotation. Later someone leaps to the conclusion that as Rama is warmed by its approach to the sun hurricanes will ensue. If we are clever, we can infer the mechanism of their production by remembering those Coriolis forces. If we are not clever, we may still be delighted to read Clarke's explanation which not only explains hurricanes in Rama but hurricanes on Earth. And in any case, we need not feel bad: the crew is not always so clever either. There are a number of phenomena that occur that could have been foreseen but were not. Having seen the phenomena, we are challenged to stop our reading and explain things; or, if we wish, we can proceed and have the explanation laid out for us. It is a very satisfying book.

The book must have been quite satisfying for Clarke as well. Many motifs that had figured almost superfluously in his earlier novels are woven skillfully into the overall fabric of *Rendezvous With Rama.* One important example of this is the motif of the man with two wives. In *The Deep Range* we follow the education of Walter Franklin from deep-sea warden to director of the Bureau of Whales. For the sake of the plot, Franklin could be nearly anyone; certainly it is symbolic enough to point out that he was first trained as an astronaut but is grounded by a fear of space ("astrophobia"). However, Clarke goes further in trying to draw out ironies: he postulates that

> Walter was married. He had a wife and family on Mars . . . [who] had spent all their lives under Martian gravity . . . so they could never come to Earth, where they would be crushed under three

46

times their normal weight.

At the same time, Walter could never go back into space *(DR,* chapter 8).

Walter worries about his lost family from time to time in the book, but finally does manage to marry an Earth woman and have two children by her as well. He never does clarify his complex feelings of near-loss/near-bigamy, and this minor but pervasive issue is unresolved at the novel's end. In *Rendezvous With Rama* Clarke proposes that Captain Norton, head of the exploration team, is also a man with "Two Wives" (chapter 7), but he seems quite reconciled to this, indeed, pleased by it. The two families, confined by gravity to Earth and Mars, send each other holiday cards, sometimes the wives chat, and Norton's only problem seems to be to make sure that his general letter home is sufficiently general to do dual duty. This state of affairs is even enhanced by the state of affairs: Norton's Chief Medical Officer is Dr. Laura Ernst, a sometime lover. In this novel the problem that nags throughout *The Deep Range* has metamorphosed into a pleasant social embellishment. One cannot help but think that with the writing of *2001* Clarke had achieved a new security and that this security is revealed in this, his next novel.

Laura Ernst is not a token female. She is shown as a fully competent officer and a fully feminine woman. In addition, the best sailor on the crew, the non-com who will guide the explorers on a makeshift raft across the Cylindrical Sea, is Sgt. Ruby Barnes. As if to put the capper on this display of sexual equality, we find Norton's dual marriage counterbalanced by one mention of

> Lieutenant Commander Mercer . . . [and] his inseparable companion, Lieutenant Joe Calvert . . . they also shared a wife back on Earth, who had borne each of them a child (chapter 10).

Clarke, despite his best conscious efforts, had always before fallen back into male chauvinism. In *The Deep Range* Walter's Earth wife gives up her career as a marine biologist to tend his children; in *A Fall of Moondust* the tour bus captain is male but the tour guide is a woman; in none of the books before *Rendezvous With Rama* does a woman really get into space with the negligible exception of the stewardess who serves Heywood Floyd on the shuttle to the Moon in *2001*. But with *2001* behind him and with his achievement of dealing squarely with the sexual implications of his monolith image complete, Clarke is finally freed of reliance on cultural stereotypes and can in this novel quite handily draw in the outlines of a society for which male chauvinism is a barbaric antiquity.

There is another image, somewhat like the monolith, that has occurred repeatedly in Clarke's work and here finally comes in for full treatment: the overhanging stairway. Whenever Clarke discusses habitable satellites, he mentions a stairway that goes from a point of lower gravity to a point of higher gravity, that is, from closer to the axis of rotation to closer to the circumference *(IS,* chapter 11; *SM,* chapter 1; *2001,* chapter 8). In Rama, the three central stairways are of this kind and they dominate the landscape whenever one looks north. Quite literally, "this stairway was as high as the Himalayas" (chapter 18). Like the earlier Clarke stairways, this one is "very steep near the axis and then slowly flattening out as it approaches the plain below" (chapter 9).

> . . . the height of the steps steadily decreased with the rising gravity. The stair had apparently been designed so that the effort required to climb it was more or less constant at every point in its long curving sweep (chapter 10).

Standing on the plain, of course, responding to a sense of "gravity" directed away from the axis, the giant stairway arching up toward the center of the world-cylinder's endplate would appear to be overhanging. But it would not in fact be doing this. The image of the overhanging stairway dramatically invalidates the idea that man is the measure of all things, and it is this image of the overhanging stairway that broods over the novel's hundreds of pages of tiny humans exploring a world vastly bigger than themselves and wholly alien.

Modern science proceeds by way of a number of assumptions, two of which are quite important for our understanding of this novel. First, experimental results are supposed to be reproducible regardless of the identity of the experimenter. Second, mechanistic—though sometimes statistical—cause-and-effect explanations are supposed to be able to generate an exhaustive description of the workings of our universe. Both these essential scientific assumptions, like the image of the overhanging stairway, show the utter inconsequence of humanity in the cosmic scheme of things. This inconsequence has been lurking behind all of Clarke's work in scientific suspense, but only in *Rendezvous With Rama,* by allowing the dominance of the staircase, does he confront it. True, one section of the novel is called "The Stairway of the Gods" (chapter 12), but that phrase is surely used metaphorically. One reason for this conclusion is the book's own ironic portrait of religion, which we will discuss shortly. The other reason is that the chapter's title image must allude to Clarke's personal experience. He dedicates the novel

> To Sri Lanka,
> where I climbed the
> stairway of the Gods

This "stairway" is a mountain path up "Adam's Peak" to a shrine. Clarke sees this journey as beautiful, but not as religious (Bernstein, p. 64). In *The Fountains of Paradise*, Adam's Peak figures decisively as a post for observation of the Space Elevator's Earth anchor in another nearby sacred mountain. In any event, *Rendezvous With Rama* dominated by the image of the overhanging stairway is unique in Clarke's work in its treatment of the subject of homocentrism.

From the very beginning of the novel, human beings are quite convinced that Rama's arrival has great significance, and indeed, it finally does prove to shake human philosophies to their foundations. Before the exploratory mission is set in operation, the characters debate the wisdom of landing on the huge cylinder:

> "But if the creatures inside Rama are . . . er . . . malevolent, will it really make the slightest difference what we do?"
> "They might ignore us if we go away."
> "What—after they've travelled billions of miles and thousands of years?" (chapter 6).

Other characters try to understand the nature of the machine that Rama apparently is:

> ". . . Rama's orbit is aimed so accurately at the solar system that coincidence seems ruled out. In fact, I'd say it's now heading much too close to the Sun for comfort . . . Perhaps there's some form of automatic terminal guidance still operating, steering Rama to the nearest suitable star ages after its builders died" (chapter 9).

When they find Rama empty of all animation, the characters still worry.

> "Even if there are no life forms aboard, it may be directed by robot mechanisms, programmed to carry out some mission—perhaps one highly disadvantageous to us . . . we must consider the question of self-defense" (chapter 19).

One of the crewmen is a member of the

> Fifth Church of Christ, Cosmonaut . . . Its members believed that Jesus Christ was a visitor from space, and an entire theology had been constructed on that assumption (chapter 12).

This homocentric notion not only conforms to the woollier speculations of Erich von Däniken *(Chariots of the Gods?* 1968) but seems to reflect parts of Clarke's own work, like the first section of *2001:* ". . . the tribe . . . . peopled the sky, not altogether inaccurately, with gods" *(2001,* chapter 6). This "Cosmo Christer" has his own explanation:

> "I believe that Rama is a cosmic Ark, sent here to save—those that

are worthy of salvation" (chapter 20).

But when Rama finally produces something "living," a "biot," a biological robot scavenger, it meets a crewman and passes him by to gather up some wrecked human equipment.

> Feeling extremely foolish, the acting representative of *Homo sapiens* watched his First Contact stride away across the Raman plain, totally indifferent to his presence (chapter 29).

Coming after such a long string of homocentric imaginings, this inauspicious meeting might seem merely ironic, but it is more than that: it picks up an earlier hint and foreshadows the novel's end. The astronomer who first spots Rama, long before anything is known about it but its course toward the sun, is suddenly chilled:

> . . . there flashed briefly through Stenton's horrified mind the memory of that timeless classic, H. G. Wells' "The Star" (chapter 2).

In that story, civilization is mindlessly demolished by an errant astronomical object and mankind itself all but destroyed. The story is told primarily from the human point of view, showing first how the approaching object is of scientific interest, then how its supposed near-passage to Earth excites people, then how its too-near-passage frightens people and then how the seas are swept up, volcanoes split open and the land masses flooded destroying almost all life. Then the story switches for its last paragraph to the viewpoint of "Martian Astronomers":

> " . . . it is astonishing what a little damage the earth . . . has sustained. All the familiar continental markings and the masses of the seas remain intact, and indeed the only difference seems to be a shrinkage of the white discoloration (supposed to be frozen water) round either pole." Which only shows how small the vastest of human catastrophes may seem, at a distance of a few million miles (1899).

Wells here deflates homocentrism with a vengeance, and Stenton's recollection of the story is our first hint of what might be going on in Clarke's novel. The encounter with the "Biot" is not merely funny.

Nonetheless, the characters continue to think of the Sun as Rama's "intended target" (chapter 38). Only when Rama begins to make course corrections, do the characters—and perhaps the readers—first realize that their homocentrism is based on pure, unscientific prejudice:

Everyone had been so certain that Rama would lose speed, so that it could be captured by the Sun's gravity and thus become a new planet of the solar system. It was doing just the opposite (chapter 44).

In Fritz Leiber's Hugo-winning *The Wanderer* (1964), an artificial planet sweeps close to the Earth, incidentally causing Wellsian catastrophe, only so as to be able to pulverize and take aboard the mass of the Moon to use as fuel in its continuing voyage. Here, when Rama begins to act,

> . . . there were definite indications that matter was flowing from the Sun *into Rama itself,* as if it was replacing the leakage and losses of ten thousand centuries in space . . . it had given a final, almost contemptuous proof of its total lack of interest in all the worlds whose peace of mind it had so rudely disturbed (chapter 45).

The Ramans

> had used the solar system as a refueling stop, a booster station—call it what you will; and had then spurned it completely, on their way to more important business. They would probably never even know that the human race existed. Such monumental indifference was worse than any insult (chapter 46).

With this penultimate thought, we can see why Clarke, why most of us, shy away from the most fundamental implications of empirical science: that humanity is of no more nor less value than a star or a grain of sand, that our intelligence is no worthier or more despicable than a plant's tropism or a computer's analog potentiality. From the standpoint of the stars, as Stapledon said again and again, we are just a brief "music," and we are only that when we provide the ears to hear it.

Clarke was only able to achieve this unique repudiation of his homocentrism after he had worked his way past the haunting imagery of *2001.* But having done that, he created a novel not only of science but of science dramatized, humanized. In the exploration of Rama, we readers feel the challenge of discovery and the exhiliration of using our minds, of encountering the new. That is one reason why the book, although it defies homocentrism, seems to uplift us.

And there is another reason that *Rendezvous With Rama* can seem to thwart human curiosity and still leave its readers feeling hopeful. Every part of the cylinder was triplicated, each of the biots was trilaterally symmetrical, even the holograms of the creatures the Earthmen believed to be Ramans had three arms and three legs. As Rama speeds out of our system, Norton is sad that he was unable to crack open the mechanical world and find its secret, for whatever mission Rama was on it must have been supremely important to warrant such effort:

> . . . he would be haunted by a sense of anticlimax and the knowledge of opportunities missed.
> So he told himself; but even then, he should have known better.
> And on far-off Earth, Dr. Carlisle Perera had as yet told no one of how he had wakened from a restless sleep with the message from his subconscious echoing in his brain:
> *The Ramans do everything in threes.*

With this last line Clarke is telling us that if one Rama came through our system, two more will follow. The universe may not care to be understood by us, but we care to understand the universe. And next time, insignificant as we are, we will be ready. *Rendezvous With Rama* is Arthur C. Clarke's most mature exploration of his constant theme of the meaning for mankind of science.

SHORT STORIES

Under the guise of science fiction, Arthur C. Clarke has written fine examples of every kind of short fiction from the ghost story to the tall tale to the lament for lost love. In addition, he has written a number of unique stories which are among the most famous in science fiction and widely read outside the field as well. "The Star" won the Hugo Award for best short story of the year in 1956. All of his short narratives published through 1958 and most published since are readily available in six collections *(Expedition to Earth, Reach For Tomorrow, Tales From The "White Hart," The Other Side of the Sky, Tales of Ten Worlds* and *The Wind From The Sun),* the contents of which are annotated in their due places in the next chapter. Here, however, we can take a more concentrated look at selected stories to better understand the wide range of Clarke's achievement in this quintessentially science fictional form.

Ghost stories abound in all cultures, the chilling tale meant for telling round a campfire. While it may at first seem hard to find a campfire in space, Clarke manages handily by setting "A Walk in the Dark" *(RFT)* on a lonely asteroid where rough-and-ready men are mining under pioneering conditions. Their camp is a small island of humanity and the rest of the planet might as well be desert, a nearly unexplored waste pocked by mysterious cavities and broken up by hills that make a man, especially at night, lose sight of far-off shelter. It would hardly be fair to tell what finally happens since so much of the power of a story like this depends on the main character's fevered imaginings, but what happens is a fitting climax indeed to the crazy fears we've all had of being followed on foot down a strange and unlit street in the wrong part of town.

Besides modifying the conventions of a form to suit science fiction, Clarke is quite able to recast the entire form. In "Who's There?" *(TTW)* Clarke has created a ghost story with a happy—indeed, a cuddly—ending. The main character is troubled by thoughts of the last man to wear the spacesuit he is occupying, a man killed in it. Adrift in space, our protagonist thinks he hears scratching noises, and then his heart drops when something brushes the back of his neck *inside the suit.* He faints, and when he revives he finds he has been rescued and removed from the spacesuit—along with the cat who had used the interior footlocker to sequester her litter.

Clarke also adds his own twists to the classic tale of time travel. In "Time's Arrow," we find two sets of scientists. One set is slowly uncovering the petrified mud tracks of a huge dinosaur being stalked by some

53

other animal. This paleontological possibility, by the way, had not been found in life before Clarke's story, but has been since. The idea of the scientists is to carefully uncover the tracks, follow them as far as need be till the two animals meet, and then see if they have found the evidence of an actual kill. The title is Sir Arthur Eddington's name for the Second Law of Thermodynamics, the law which states, in one form, that water won't flow uphill. In other words, there's no turning back the clock, no putting smashed radios back together, and so forth. Put technically, all activity in all closed systems yields an increase in entropy, disorder. The second set of scientists is pursuing a highly secret project which, it turns out, is attempting to create a local field in which Time's Arrow is reversed. As the senior paleontologist drives his jeep toward the physicists' installation, the huge building explodes. When the paleontologist's assistants finish uncovering the petrified tracks, they find that their dinosaur, in the far past, had turned and trampled a jeep. The paradoxes just won't go away.

With a somewhat different twist, "All the Time in the World" *(OSS)* follows a thief engaged by someone from the future to steal Earth's treasures, a job made easy by wearing a wristlet he is given that speeds him up thousands of times. He appears to himself to be functioning normally, however, while everyone else seems to have stopped. We finally discover that the futurians are not so much stealing mankind's art as rescuing it. It seems that time travel is only possible at special moments of terrific energetic tension, such as when a world blows up. At the end of the story the thief is sitting alone on a curb pondering his choices: he can keep wearing the wristlet and live out what will seem to him a normal life amid a frozen humanity or he can take off the wristlet, see the world restored to its now-desireable norm, only to see it immolated within minutes. In leaving us with such images of paradox or ambivalence, Clarke takes the short story form and enriches it immeasurably, making of a few minutes entertainment something that remains vivid in the mind for later contemplation.

In "The Songs of Distant Earth" *(OSS)*, Clarke also creates a haunting image, this one much like the vision of falling snow at the end of Joyce's "The Dead" (1914). Clarke's story is one of love on a far-off and pastoral planet, an idyllic Earth colony which has been out of touch since its founding three hundred years earlier. Our focal couple have grown up together and want no one but each other; they expected and are expected to marry. But one day strangers come down from the sky. Earth has continued its colonizations, always sending out hibernating adventurers within the bowels of robot-controlled ships. When a malfunction occurs that the robots cannot handle, a skeleton crew is automatically revived in the ship parked in orbit around the older colony. To the girl, these strangers bring the romance of legendary Earth, of a place of wonders and the race's youth. She falls in love irresistibly with a young engineer. He, in turn, whether he should or not, falls in love with her. The crew stay for a few weeks while they do their work and the fisherlad, her fiancé, falls into ever-greater desperation, but his pacific culture forbids a violent confrontation. When finally the time comes for departure, the girl wants to be taken along, put into suspended animation for the long voyage so that she can awaken with her new love at its end. But he takes her to the ship and shows her the freezer lockers ranked with hundreds of corpse-like colonists—including the engineer's pregnant wife. As the ship leaves, the girl and fisherlad are together again, intending again to marry, but with the vision in both their minds of the frozen Earthman who will forever come between them and who will revive to begin his own new life long after they are dead.

In a much lighter vein, Clarke is, perhaps surprisingly, one of the masters of short fiction humor. Since the joke often turns on an unexpected outcome, it would not be sporting to discuss many of these stories in detail, but a few of the most famous will convey the spectrum of Clarke's comedy which is sometimes subtle and sometimes poignant, but quite often just delightfully silly. In "Neutron Tide" (WFS) we get an expert discussion of the huge gravitational forces associated with a collapsed star, forces so powerful that at close range they exert a readily perceptible gravity gradient. The story merely tells of a rocket ship that came too close to a neutron star and was ripped apart by this terrible gravitational field, practically atomized, with no identifiable remains except for a single, horribly deformed wrench: the now famous "star-mangled spanner."

In "History Lesson" (EE) we follow the researches of amphibious Venusian scientists of the far future as they try to reconstruct Earth life by examination of the very few artifacts that have survived both atomic war and repeated glaciation. The most troubling is an apparently clear strip of celluloid. Finally they recognize this as a faded series of pictures, learn to bring out the detail and project it. They are amazed to see how Earthlings careen about, knocking into things with no apparent ill effect, how they stumble over each other, how they use their three-fingered hands. Unfortunately, no one is able to learn enough of the language to translate the final symbols that come in the last frames: "A Walt Disney Production."

Perhaps Clarke's most famous humorous stories are those collected in *Tales From The "White Hart."* This volume is set up much like *The Canterbury Tales,* a succession of humorous pieces strung on a humorous framework. The context story concerns the weekly meetings of scientists, science fiction writers, and editors at the "White Hart" tavern, informal gatherings where story ideas are swapped and refined and tall tales are told. The undisputed master of that form is one Harry Purvis who reports —or concocts—each of the fifteen wild-eyed stories embedded in the work. (One more Harry Purvis story, "Let There Be Light," is collected in *Tales of Ten Worlds.*) Each of these stories is based on some scientific oddity or impossibility which Purvis claims he has seen in action, like sonic interference creating a bomb ("Silence Please") or ice-making equipment used by the California Chamber of Commerce to create artificial icebergs to float at Florida and ruin their tourist trade ("Cold War"). Each of these stories is witty and pleasant in itself, both for the central idea and for the treatment, but taken as a whole the volume conveys the lovely sense that somewhere good fellowship and jolly conversation still prevail. If only one could find the "White Hart."

One of these stories concerns a man cursed with snoring. At his wife's urging, he goes to his mad scientist relative for help and is helped—by a potion that keeps him permanently awake. When the difficulties of that are recognized, the scientist overcures the problem by concocting a potion that puts the sufferer into a deep and permanent sleep, creating yet another problem. The solution can be read in this story called, naturally enough, "Sleeping Beauty."

Many of Clarke's stories pay homage to earlier writings. In the previous case the fairy tale reference adds a bit of irony. In other cases the reference may be merely fortuitous. "Out of the Cradle, Endlessly Orbiting" *(TWW)* clearly echoes Walt Whitman's "Out of the Cradle, Endlessly Rocking," but an echo is all we get. In Whitman the cradle is the sea, the literal subject of a poem about poetic inspiration, while in Clarke the cradle predicts the climactic lunar birth of a baby at the story's end. In "The Food of the Gods" *(WFS)*, Clarke has reused a title from a Wells novel (1904) which is similar only in that both foods are created by scientists. In Wells' case the food induces giantism and the superior eaters are shunned by humanity at large; in the quite different case of Clarke, the public clamors for this best of all possible artificial comestibles—which turns out to be chemically indistinguishable from human meat. More appropriately, "Maelstrom II" *(WFS)* picks up Poe's trick from "A Descent into the Maelstrom" (1841) of having a hero caught in a whirlpool save himself by clinging to a caisson that floats on the swirling interior surface—except Clarke sets his circle not within the ocean but around the Moon. And Clarke adds a few extra astrophysical tricks of his own at the end.

Perhaps Clarke's greatest response to an earlier work is his "The Star" *(OSS)*. As discussed in the last chapter, Wells' own story of this name shows how trivial are the desires of humanity when viewed from a cosmic perspective. In this reply to Wells, Clarke begins his tale "three thousand light-years [from] the Vatican," but, thanks to the "Transfinite Drive," only a thousand years from now. The main character is a Jesuit astrophysicist who examines a stellar cloud and realizes that he is observing the remains of a supernova. He finds a planet which must have been far removed from that cataclysm, and on this planet the lonely "monument . . . [of] a civilization that knew it was about to die [and] had made its last bid for immortality."

> Many of us had seen the ruins of ancient civilizations on other worlds, but they had never affected us so profoundly. This tragedy was unique. It is one thing for a race to fail and die, as nations and cultures have done on Earth. But to be destroyed in the full flower of its achievement, leaving no survivors—how could that be reconciled with the mercy of God?

For better or worse, the reconciliation follows from the laws of physics, for the Jesuit is able to calculate that the star went supernova six thousand years earlier, so that its light was bright in the sky of Earth three thousand years earlier. In the last line, the physicist wonders with heavy heart, "What was the need to give these people to the fire, that the symbol of their passing might shine above Bethlehem?"

Although this story obviously explores philosophical issues, asking even through its homocentrism if there is such a thing as absolute good or absolute evil, still the narrative flow depends on particular scientific detail, a knowledge in this case of the kind of event that a supernova is and of the time necessary for light to travel astronomical distances. Many of Clarke's stories are devoted primarily to the exposition of scientific detail. "Take a Deep Breath" (OSS) does little more than explain how one could cross a vacuum without a spacesuit and then show it happen; "Jupiter Five," (RFT) which is another of Clarke's tales of the relics of early alien visitors to our solar system, turns on a threat which sounds fearsome but is in fact trivial—once one understands the mechanics of relative orbital velocities; and "I Remember Babylon" (TTW) is basically the exposition of someone's scheme to use Clarke's own idea of comsats to brainwash the whole of America by attracting a viewership through uncensored pornography and treating them to political propaganda originated in China and beamed from the skies. But sometimes, no matter the importance of science to the story, the result is one of those images that will not go away, that seem to capture something permanent about the human condition. In "Robin Hood, F.R.S." (OSS) a lunar exploring party is stranded and cannot be saved for a long time, but one supply load can be dropped to them. Unfortunately, the vital capsule lands on a towering cliff, much too steep to climb. The endangered people, since they are on the airless moon, have no flying craft. Finally they solve their problem by making a sophisticated, but essentially ordinary bow and arrow from the wreckage of their equipment. With this, they can launch a rope to the capsule, climb up and lower the life-giving supplies. " . . . that incongruous spectacle of the space-suited figure, gleaming in the last rays of the setting sun, as it drew its bow against the sky" is an emblem for human ingenuity and self-reliance and the wisdom of preserving the past no matter how advanced we may want to think ourselves. This is Clarke using science to create lasting fiction.

Another group of Clarke's stories are famous in their own right but particularly well known because they show the germ of his later work. Most prominent in this group are "The Sentinel" and "Expedition to Earth," *(EE)* both of which give early discussion to ideas that are central to *2001.* In cases like his use of the monolith image, it may well be that Clarke is in some unconscious sense compelled to return to the same materials until he has dealt with them in a fully satisfying manner. But in the case of certain scientific ideas, like those in the stories just mentioned or those exploring the social implications of communications satellites, we can see the products of a mind captivated by materials of great intrinsic interest. After a lifetime of dealing with these materials, Clarke both as fiction writer and as science writer understands them as well as anyone in the world.

There are four more stories which one ought to make special mention of for they have become a part of a more general literature. "Rescue Party" *(RFT),* in one sense Clarke's first story, is still considered by some to be his best *(RFT,* Preface). In this tale we follow the efforts of superior aliens to reach and save the primitive civilization they know to exist on Earth. Clarke's device of doubling for richness runs throughout the story as the scouting parties, sent to find the presumably cowering Earthlings, themselves get embroiled in difficulty and rescue parties need to be sent out for them. Finally the aliens realize that the people of Earth had abandoned their planet. The aliens' powerful telescopes turn away from the sun and spot a massive squadron of huge chemical rockets heading toward the stars. The alien captain speaks:

> "This is the race . . . that has known radio for only two centuries —the race that we believed had crept in the heart of its planet . . . Yes, they dared to use rockets to bridge interstellar space! . . . We had better be polite to them. After all, we only outnumber them about a thousand million to one."
> Rugon laughed at his captain's little joke.
> Twenty years afterward, the remark didn't seem funny.

This is Clarke expressing his homocentrism with a wit and enthusiasm that can't help but please us all.

"Superiority" *(EE)* is a story of interstellar war. One race is winning because they are richer, more numerous and more advanced. But then the head of their military research and development effort dies and is replaced by a real innovator. Each of his successive innovations is more astounding than the last, each a more perfect weapon, and each costs more and more in time and money as its deployment requires ever greater excesses of retooling. Meanwhile the other side nibbles away at the innovating culture by fighting doggedly on with their trusty old methods. The story is carried along briskly by the imagination of the sundry weapons and the paradoxical progress of superiority yielding decline. Finally the originally powerful side is brought dazedly to its knees. "We were defeated by one thing only —by the inferior science of our enemies." Clarke has expressed himself as particularly pleased that this story has been used as required reading at M.I.T.

"The Possessed" *(RFT)* takes the Stapledonian idea of a group mind and follows it lyrically from the mind's point of view. The ethereal group mind comes to Earth in search of creatures sufficiently intelligent to use for embodiment, but arrives too early in Earth's history. Fearing its own demise, the mind splits itself, one half to search again among the stars, the other to await the vagaries of Earthly evolution. Periodically the Earth-bound half is to return to the mountain valley where the split occurred to await the spacefarer's possible return with good news. The years pass. The Earthly mind infiltrates a likely tree-dwelling species. The mountains subside and the valley is flooded. As the ages go on without the emergence of intelligence, the separated parts of the group mind lose their capacities, remembering only their appointed meeting. It all comes to these last lines:

> Obeying an urge whose meaning they had never known, the doomed legions of the lemmings were finding oblivion beneath the waves.

Clarke's most famous story, and the one he chose as the title story for his own selection of his best short fiction, is "The Nine Billion Names of God" *(OSS).* This story presents a direct confrontation between Western science and Eastern mysticism. A group of Buddhist monks has come to believe that the purpose of the human race is to enumerate the names of God and that once they accomplish this the world can end. In a special alphabet they have devised, they have calculated that the total number of these names is nine billion. For centuries they have been laboring along, constructing the allowable permutations and combinations, recording these and working on. But the current lama sees that the work of the brotherhood can be aided by a properly programmed computer. Two

American engineers are sent to the mountaintop lamasery to supervise the computer's functioning. The lamasery has its own electrical generator, it turns out, to keep the prayer wheels functioning. The Americans are quite sure, of course, that the project is sheer folly. They fear that when nothing happens at the completion of the three month computer program, the monks will feel cheated and angry, so they arrange to leave on the last day, hoping to make it by mountain pony down to the airfield in the valley before the machine finishes writing God's names. They look down at their destination, an hour off: "The battered old DC3 lay at the end of the runway like a tiny silver cross." As they near the plain an hour later, something happens.

> "Look," whispered Chuck, and George lifted his eyes to heaven. (There is always a last time for everything.)
> Overhead, without any fuss, the stars were going out.

For forty years Arthur C. Clarke has written *science* fiction, but it has been, first and always, *fiction*. This means that what Clarke writes may appear to be about science, appear to be about numbers, appear to be about ideas, but in fact at bottom whatever Clarke writes is about people and that means that it is about the human spirit. In his parenthetical penultimate sentence Clarke lets us share a point of view fundamentally at peace with mankind but speaking to it from a loftier and more knowledgeable vantage. When he applauds human curiosity despite the cold factuality of science, as in *Rendezvous With Rama,* when he glories in man's chaotic energies for change, as in *The City and the Stars,* and when he celebrates even mankind's passing in *Childhood's End* or *2001* or "The Nine Billion Names of God," he creates that "brief music" that is man. In over thirty different languages, millions have heard that music and been moved.

ANNOTATED BIBLIOGRAPHY OF FICTION

This alphabetical listing states briefly the nature of each of Clarke's volumes of fiction, including the contents of his most important collections with the original years of publication of the stories. Discussion of almost all his fictions occur whenever relevant in the chapters centering on his biography, his four greatest novels and his short stories. This compilation, rather than making comparisons, deals with each volume in its own right. The annotations are short, designed for ready reference so that they can be used as reminders of what each book is about. The index will give those pages on which a book or story is mentioned in the body of this guide.

Across the Sea of Stars. New York: Harcourt Brace, 1959. Collection including *CE, EL* and eighteen short stories drawn from *EE, TWH* and *RFT.*

Against the Fall of Night. New York: Gnome Press, 1953. Novel. Alvin is the first child born in a static city-environment in thousands of years. His irrepressible curiosity leads him first to break out of the city, then to discover humanity's pastoral branch, and finally to cause these collateral groups to reinvigorate each other. His rediscovery of a buried spaceship from the golden technological past allows him to tour the relics of galactic empire and draw to Earth a creature of pure mentality who will help mankind regain its past and fare forward again. This is a shorter early version of *The City and the Stars.*

The Best of Arthur C. Clarke. Ed. Angus Wells, London: Sidgwick and Jackson, 1973. Short stories drawn from magazines and earlier collections.

Childhood's End. New York: Ballantine, 1953; London: Sidgwick and Jackson, 1954. Novel. An alien race comes to Earth, preempting human war and restricting humanity to this one planet. The Overlords provide technology and peace so that numerous different utopias can emerge, but no true intellectual progress occurs. Finally, in an access of the paranormal, all the children of humanity achieve "Total Breakthrough," transcending *Homo sapiens* and becoming participants in an immensely powerful group mind that floats off to join with the Overmind as the Earth is destroyed.

The City and the Stars. New York: Harcourt Brace; London: Muller, 1956. Novel. A much expanded version of *Against the Fall of Night,* this later novel adds an unsuccessful love interest and some even more amazing thought-responsive machinery, especially in the city of Diaspar, making Alvin's philosophical breakthrough that much more dramatic by comparison.

The Deep Range. New York: Harcourt Brace, and London, Muller, 1957. Novel. This is a highly detailed and captivating exposition of future ocean farming, including plankton crops and whale herding. There are numerous vivid scenes of deepsea operations, submarine encounters with whales and giant squid, and sometimes fatal catastrophes beneath the waves. The main character begins as an emotional cripple, psychologically wounded by having drifted off from his ship in space and believing for a few hours that he was beyond rescue. He works his way up through all the jobs in the Bureau of Whales, herding them, training new "whaleboys," finally administering the bureau. He ends the novel as a happily married man who has been converted philosophically to using the rather intelligent whales not for flesh but for milk.

Dolphin Island: A Story of the People of the Sea. New York: Holt Rinehart, and London, Gollancz, 1963. In this juvenile novel, Johnny Clinton runs away from his guardian Aunt Martha, is shipwrecked, and then saved by dolphins who pull him on a piece of flotsam to the island research station where Professor Kazan is investigating dolphins whom he thinks of as "the People of the Sea." The novel weaves together reef exploration, speculation about dolphin intelligence and training based on John Lilly's work, and a few exciting sequences including a hurricane and surf-boarding in swollen seas with the intelligent cooperation of the dolphins. The emotional progress follows Johnny's establishment of a home on the island and his virtual adoption by the professor.

Earthlight. New York: Ballantine; London: Muller, 1955. Novel. Earth's colonies have formed a Federation which covets mineral riches believed to be buried deep in the Moon. The Lunar colony, presumably part of Earth, is leaking strategic information to the Federation. Bertram Sadler, accountant, is pressed into counterintelligence service to uncover the source of the leaks using an audit of the Lunar Observatory as his cover. There is a great deal 'of excellent astronomical and mechanical detail and some superb speculation about living under pressure domes, "pressure mining," and laser weaponry. Narratively weak, however, in that Sadler is ineffectual and the happy outcome is as much a product of luck as intelligence.

Expedition to Earth. New York: Ballantine, 1953; London, Sidgwick and Jackson, 1954. A collection of short stories containing the following:
"Second Dawn" (1951): a typical tale of two races profiting by mutual interaction, but unusual in that neither of the races is *Homo sapiens.*
" 'If I Forget Thee, Oh Earth . . .' " (1951): a lyrical lament from

the colonized Moon for the Earth made uninhabitable by nuclear war.

"Breaking Strain" (1949): an intense character study of two men on a disabled spaceship with sufficient resources for only one to survive.

"History Lesson" (1949): a comic tale about Venusian scientists of the far future trying to reconstruct Earth life from a few post-nuclear artifacts.

"Superiority" (1951): an ironic exposition of the way a military research establishment can be too clever for its own good.

"Exile of the Eons" (1950): a Hitler-like dictator from our time escapes retribution by self-induced suspended animation only to revive in the future for a confrontation with a Gandhi-like philosopher who finds him unworthy of life.

"Hide and Seek" (1949): a lone astronaut on the surface of tiny Phobos scuttles about trying to elude the pursuit of a space cruiser with its weapons designed for much larger prey.

"Expedition to Earth" (1953): superior aliens land on Earth at the dawn of primate development and leave tools with the hope that this gift will induce the evolution of intelligence.

"Loophole" (1946): Martians interdict Earthlings' use of rockets and watch smugly from their Lunar observation post until mankind suddenly launches a counterblow in a most unexpected way.

"Inheritance" (1948): a man with a history of premonitory dreams inaccurately foresees his own demise—but his fate is passed on to his son.

"The Sentinel" (1951): often called the first version of *2001*, a lunar explorer discovers an obviously artificial and alien pyramid on the Moon and tampers with it, thus setting off the alarm that humanity is on the move.

A Fall of Moondust. New York: Harcourt Brace; London, Gollancz, 1961. Novel. A superbly told tale of a mixed group trapped on a sightseeing tour beneath a "sea" of lunar dust so fine that it flows like a liquid. The cast of characters is as stereotypically drawn as in any disaster movie but they are treated with exceptional wit. In addition, the scientific challenge the book presents the reader of trying to think through the physical problems before the rescuers can is as satisfying as any good whodunit.

The Fountains of Paradise. New York: Harcourt Brace, and London, Gollancz, 1979. The major action of this novel of technological detail is the planning and construction of a forty thousand kilometer Space Elevator to bridge humanity's way to the stars. Woven into the story of Vannevar Morgan, the engineer hero, is a spiritual level

63

focusing in the past on the legendary rulers of Sri Lanka and in the future on the impact made on humanity's self-image by contact with Starglider, an ancient automated space probe on a transgalactic mission of exploration for its alien creators. Balancing scientific enthusiasm and spiritual optimism, this novel offers both engrossing exposition and profession of the author's faith.

From the Ocean, From the Stars. New York: Harcourt Brace, 1962. Collection including *DR, CS* and *OSS.*

Glide Path. New York: Harcourt Brace, 1963; London, Sidgwick and Jackson, 1969. Novel. Clarke's only non-science fiction novel, and perhaps the only novel written about radar, this is a rather mechanical attempt to weave some moderately dramatic incidents into a unified work. The book offers some interest not only in its uniqueness but in its typically polished descriptions and in its faint hint of autobiographical veracity.

Imperial Earth. New York: Harcourt Brace; London: Gollancz, 1976. This novel is divided into parts, each of which has independent interest in the social and physical conditions it depicts. The opening on Titan, a moon of Saturn, explores the implications of "corridor culture" on a world of light gravity with an atmosphere of unbreathable hydrocarbons. The second section gives us a visual tour of the inner half of the solar system and life aboard a passenger rocket as our main character makes his once-in-a-lifetime trip to Earth to participate as his world's representative at America's quincentennial celebrations. The major part of the book is set on a future Earth of low population, technological perfection and, except for occasional boredom, utopian social conditions. Our hero, a clone, not only must speak to the world but must also reproduce himself using Earth's technology to carry on his family dynasty. He must also establish a personal network of contacts who will serve as his future power base, and he must find a new basis for Titan's economy since its old basis is about to become a victim of technological obsolescence. Throughout, we follow our hero's psychological engagement with a fellow Titan who was his admired older friend as a boy, his rival in love, and finally, he suspects, his political enemy. Everything, the scientific and social details and the politics and the psychology, finally gets pulled together at the end with a satisfying sense of completion.

Islands in the Sky. Philadelphia: Winston; London: Sidgwick and Jackson, 1952. This juvenile novel follows the experiences of a boy who wins a trip to an artificial satellite used, among other things, as a training ground for space cadets. He parlays this luck into a rocket trip, a space walk, a trip to a geostationary comsat, a rescue mission, participation in a big budget feature film and a fly-by of the moon. Clearly the plot is not much more than an excuse to demonstrate all these wonders, but the demonstration itself is masterful even more than twenty years after Sputnik.

The Lion of Commare. Novel. First book publication in *The Lion of Comarre, and Against the Fall of Night.* New York: Harcourt Brace, 1968; London: Gollancz, 1970. Some of the world's great geniuses have disappeared over the generations into the ancient city of Comarre fenced away inside the "Wild Lands." Dick Peyton crosses into restricted territory, befriends a lion, and enters Comarre which turns out to be a self-perpetuating city that seduces visitors into lethargy by the mechanical perfection of "the ancient dream of the Lotus Eaters." Like Androcles, Dick is saved in the nick of time by his lion's intervention, frees for all mankind's use the knowledge that went into building Comarre, and manages to destroy the threat the city itself poses. This novella has more the atmosphere of a fairy tale than any of Clarke's other work.

The Nine Billion Names of God. New York: Harcourt Brace, 1967. This collection of Clarke's own favorites among his stories draws its contents from his five earlier collections: *Expedition to Earth, Reach For Tomorrow, Tales From The "White Hart," The Other Side of the Sky,* and *Tales of Ten Worlds.* The stories are annotated elsewhere in this listing under the title under which each was first collected. The stories are listed here (with their sources) so that one can see which of his works Clarke himself most wanted to keep before the public: "The Nine Billion Names of God" *(OSS),* "I Remember Babylon" *(TTW),* "Trouble With Time" *(TTW),* "Rescue Party" *(RFT),* "The Curse" *(RFT),* "Summertime on Icarus" *(TTW),* "Dog Star" *(TTW),* "Hide and Seek" *(EE),* "Out of the Sun" *(OSS),* "The Wall of Darkness" *(OSS),* "No Morning After" *(OSS),* "The Possessed" *(RFT),* "Death and the Senator" *(TTW),* "Who's There?" *(TTW),* "Before Eden" *(TTW),* "Superiority" *(EE),* "A Walk in the Dark" *(RFT),* "The Call of the Stars" *(OSS),* "The Reluctant Orchid" *(TWH),* "Encounter at Dawn" *(EE),* " 'If I Forget Thee, Oh Earth . . .' " *(EE),* "Patent Pending" *(TWH),* "The Sentinel" *(EE),* "Transience" *(OSS),* and "The Star" *(OSS).*

The Other Side of the Sky. New York: Harcourt Brace, 1958; London: Gollancz, 1963. A collection of short stories contain the following:
"The Nine Billion Names of God" (1953): Western science confronting Eastern religion in Clarke's most famous story.
"Refugee" (1955): a likeable young crown prince stows away on a space ship.

"The Other Side of the Sky" (1957): a group of very short stories linked by their common setting on artificial satellites. Included are "Special Delivery," about a plan to sneak goodies over the weight allowance to a satellite crew; "Feathered Friend," about a bird who warns the satellite crew of a gas problem as birds once did in mines; "Take a Deep Breath," about crossing a vacuum without a spacesuit; "Freedom of Space," about a man who decides to throw over a good career on Earth for the privacy and weightlessness of life on a satellite; "Passer-by," about a love-struck spacer out without permission who fails to report an alien object; and "The Call of the Stars," about the way danger and adventure take sons from their fathers.

"The Wall of Darkness" (1949): on a world with very odd geometry a man of vision dares to explore the unknown, only to find it even odder than he had ever imagined.

"Security Check" (1957): recalling Cleve Cartmill's actual questioning during World War II for having successfully described the making of an atomic bomb in his story "Deadline," this tale has an inventor protagonist who unwittingly infringes on extraterrestrial secrets and is hauled off for questioning by real aliens.

"No Morning After" (1954): a telepathic race foreseeing the end of the world tries to break through to mankind with a message, but the only mind sensitive to their call is a drunk who thinks he's hallucinating.

"Venture to the Moon" (1956-57): another group of very short stories, this one linked by a common concern with the first expedition to the Moon. Included are "The Starting Line," about the friendly rivalry among the American, English and Russian captains of the three pioneering vessels; "Robin Hood, F.R.S." about how comparatively primitive technology can save the day when sophisticated technology proves too clever by half; "Green Fingers," about the pioneering botanist who breeds a plant to tame the Moon, and dies for his science; "All That Glitters," about the relative values people find in the beautiful and the rare; "Watch This Space," about the biggest advertising coup in history; and "A Question of Residence," about how even lunar explorers can be swayed by Earthly matters of finance.

"Publicity Campaign" (1956): a huge publicity campaign for an invasion movie stirs up so much xenophobia that when real aliens land with the friendliest of intentions, Earth's population meets them with violence—and invites the destruction of the world.

"All the Time in the World" (1951): a man is granted the gift of a tremendously speeded up mode of life so that everyone appears frozen to him; he can live out his days in apparent normalcy as a lone inhabitant of a petrified world or he can throw away the "gift" and return to the normal world he yearns for—but which he knows will explode within very few normal minutes.

"Cosmic Casanova" (1958): a space-going ladies' man courts a gorgeous woman by videophone, only to discover on his arrival that the camera, even without meaning it, sometimes lies.

"The Star" (1955): an answer to Wells' anti-homocentrism in his story of the same name, this tale asserts humanity's centrality in God's scheme of things, but leaves us wondering if this special position is just.

"Out of the Sun" (1958): a freak, monstrous prominence exploded out of the sun turns out to harbor a world-sized creature wholly different from mankind, and doomed to die in the coldness of space.

"Transcience" (1949): the history of humanity reduced to three snapshots of man-ape, mankind, and man gone.

"The Songs of Distant Earth" (1958): a pastoral lament for lost love.

Prelude to Mars. New York: Harcourt Brace, 1965. Collection including PS, SM and sixteen short stories drawn from EE, RFT and TWH.

Prelude to Space. New York: World Editions, 1951; London: Sidgwick and Jackson, 1953. An early novel that deals with the preparations leading up to the first attempt at manned flight to the moon. There's a lot of scientific detail, often prescient but sometimes just wrong, and a very thin plot intended to support a technological optimism that few people still find convincing.

Reach For Tomorrow. New York: Ballantine, 1956; London: Gollancz, 1962. A collection of short stories containing the following:

"Rescue Party" (1946): aliens do their darnedest to save the inhabitants of a doomed Earth, only to discover that they are the ones who may need saving.

"A Walk in the Dark" (1950): a classic ghost story set on a mining asteroid.

"The Forgotten Enemy" (1953): a lone Londoner observes the final advances of mankind's final foe, which turns out not to be a living thing at all.

"Technical Error" (1950): a matter-antimatter story in which an intrepid scientist bombs out.

"The Parasite" (1953): a telepathic leech takes over a man's mind and induces him to suicide, just as it transfers itself to the mind of his previously doubting friend.

"The Fires Within" (1949): the discovery of a much denser form of life within the Earth itself.

"The Awakening" (1951): a man who finds utopia too boring decides to escape to the future via suspended animation; the future is not what he expected.

"Trouble With the Natives" (1951): a comic story in which bumbling extraterrestrials on Earth can't get anyone to believe they want to meet Earth's leader.

"The Curse" (1953): elegiac conflation of the modern curse of atomic war and the centuries old curse Shakespeare had carved on his gravestone.

"Time's Arrow" (1952): a scientist uncovering petrified dinosaur tracks is caught in a time-reverse field and trampled by his quarry.

"Jupiter Five" (1953): one man trying to preserve the statue of an ancient alien found in an artificial world previously thought to be a moon of Jupiter bluffs a carpetbagger with abandonment in orbit—good astrophysical detail.

"The Possessed" (1952): a group mind stranded on Earth millions of years ago takes up residence in a species it hopes will evolve intelligence but which evolves something else instead.

Rendezvous With Rama. New York: Harcourt Brace, 1973; London: Pan Books, 1974. This novel is unique in Clarke's fiction in that it supports an anti-homocentric view of the universe. With the characters, the reader makes a suspenseful and detailed exploration of an artificial planet that invades our system for purposes unknown. Our ideas of ourselves as well as our slide rules are challenged by the complexity of the reported setting. This is the only work ever to have won all four major science fiction awards.

The Sands of Mars. London: Sidgwick and Jackson, 1951; New York: Gnome Press, 1952. This novel quite successfully conjoins scientific detail concerning spaceflight and life under pressure domes with a love story, a tale of a long-lost son and the fight of a culture hero to nurture his world. There are delightful scenes of first contact with cute Martians and some imaginative ideas about how one might make Mars finally habitable for humans.

Tales From The "White Hart." New York: Ballantine, 1957. A collection of comic tall tales linked by the voice of Harry Purvis, their teller. The volume contains the following:

"Silence Please" (1954): sonic interference creates a bomb.

"Big Game Hunt" (1954): brain waves are broadcast in an effort to capture alive a giant squid.

"Patent Pending" (1954): electrical stimulation of the various brain centers is taken to the extreme of an erotograph.

"Armaments Race" (1954): in an effort to produce ever more convincing props for science fiction movies, a down-at-the-heels inventor comes up with functional ray guns.

"Critical Mass" (1957): a cloud rising from a truck accident near a reactor seems to be of radioactive gasses, but turns out to be something comically different.

"The Ultimate Melody" (1956): an inventor uses computer analysis to discover and purify the element that makes certain melodies stick in the mind so that he can produce the most hypnotic melody of all—which then drives him mad.

"The Pacifist" (1956): a computer programmed to run a national military establishment discovers a way to stop war altogether.

"The Next Tenants" (1956): termites, once helped by being given tools to overcome the evolutionary threshold now restraining them, may progress again and inherit the Earth.

"Moving Spirit" (1956): a tall tale of a tall tale concocted by a scientist to help out a friend justifiably accused of running an illegal still.

"The Man Who Ploughed the Sea" (1956): a scheme to remove minerals from sea water not only captures the greed of a notable exploiter of natural resources but embroils him finally in protecting the land.

"The Reluctant Orchid" (1956): a timid horticulturist who fears his butch aunt cultivates a meat-eating plant right out of Wells' "The Strange Orchid" (1897) only to find that the plant fears his aunt as well.

"Cold War" (1956): a scheme by the California Chamber of Commerce to ruin Florida's competition for tourists by landing icebergs on Miami Beach fortuitously helps the U.S. in an encounter in the international Cold War.

"What Goes Up" (1955): a sphere of anti-gravity, through complex physics delightful to read, makes for a horizontal mountain.

"Sleeping Beauty" (1957): a modern fairy tale in which sleeping potions, and waking potions, are used in an attempt to cure chronic snoring.

"The Defenestration of Ermintrude Inch" (1956): a story about a woman who just talked too much—and might well be Harry's wife.

Tales of Ten Worlds. New York: Harcourt Brace, 1962; London: Gollancz, 1963. A collection of short stories containing the following:

"I Remember Babylon" (1960): a Chinese scheme to brainwash the world by broadcasting uncensorable pornography from communications satellites.

"Summertime on Icarus" (1962): tense story of a last minute rescue from an asteroid going too near the sun.

"Out of the Cradle, Endlessly Orbiting . . ." (1959): technical achievements pale beside the symbolism of the first extraterrestrial human birth.

"Who's There?" (1958): a comic ghost story about misplaced fear in a spacesuit.

"Hate" (1961): a gripping tale of cold-blooded revenge with a wrenching surprise ending.

"Into the Comet" (1960): when a computer fails and strands a spacecraft investigating within a comet's tail, the day is saved by a makeshift abacus.

"An Ape About the House" (1962): a funny story of a hired "super-chimp" who turns out to be a worse homemaker than the mistress of the house but a much better artist in oils—if she can use her feet.

"Saturn Rising" (1961): lyric story of a boy's dream of space travel finally embodied in his old age by creation of a magnificent tourist hotel on a moon of Saturn.

"Let There Be Light" (1957): a funny story about inducing an auto accident with a flash of light—hence a "death ray."

"Death and the Senator" (1961): as death approaches, private joys come to overshadow public activity so that the protagonist even refuses the miracle of medicine offered him to preserve his new-found inner peace.

"Trouble With Time" (1960): a thief has everything about his robbery figured correctly—except the International Date Line.

"Before Eden" (1961): an expedition of humans finds utterly primitive life on Venus and unwittingly leaves contaminants that wipe it out before it can evolve.

"A Slight Case of Sunstroke" (1958): the outcome of a Latin American soccer game—and of a Latin American *coup d'état*—hangs on thousands of fans using their silvered game programs to reflect sunlight into the eyes of the referee, and incinerate him.

"Dog Star" (1962): an astronomer owes his life to a dog sensitive to Earthquakes—and to the dog's spirit that protects him from Moonquakes.

"The Road to the Sea" (1950): mankind splits into a static, pastoral branch and a spacefaring branch, but the latter return after 5,000 years to rescue their cousins from impending doom.

2001: A Space Odyssey. New York: New American Library; London: Hutchinson, 1968. This novel is Clarke's most famous. In the first section we see a monolith teach man-apes the rudiments of the use of tools so that they are nudged along the evolutionary road to intelligence. In the next section, set in the year 2001, men discover a monolith on the Moon and set out to track the signals it has sent to their intended receiver. Subsequent sections show routine space flight, the disastrous mental breakdown of the conscious shipboard computer Hal, the sole surviving astronaut's capture by higher intelligences and his enforced tour through the far regions of the cosmos and finally his transformation into the almost infinitely capable but still young Star-Child, a super-creature pondering over ways to help Earth.

The Wind From The Sun. New York: Harcourt Brace; London: Gollancz, 1972. A collection of short stories containing the following:

"The Food of the Gods" (1971): in an era of synthetic food, the world's new favorite turns out to have a very familiar flavor.

"Maelstrom II" (1961): an orbital remake of Poe's famous story of escape with a few new twists added.

"The Shining Ones" (1963): an encounter with truly giant squids which turn out to be intelligent.

"The Wind from the Sun" (1963): lyric tale of a race among vast flimsy sailships driven from Earth to the Moon by the pressure of light.

"The Secret" (1963): Moon colonists are afraid to let the people on Earth know that the reduced lunar gravity will triple human lifespan.

"The Last Command" (1963): after a devastating atomic war, the recorded voice of the President of the United States enjoins the survivors to stop retaliating and to abjure war for the sake of whatever humanity remains.

"Dial F for Frankenstein" (1963): when the total number of networked connections in the global telephone system approaches that of the neurons in a human brain, the human race suddenly has a new consciousness to deal with.

"Reunion" (1964): a story of humanity split into two branches and then rejoined, but with a clever racial twist.

"Playback" (1964): an electromagnetically stored mind fails to maintain its pattern and dissipates—told from the mind's point of view.

"The Light of Darkness" (1964): a scientist topples a government by lasering out the eyes of the dictator.

"The Longest Science Fiction Story Ever Told" (1965): a clever tale constructed in the form of two mirrors, one reflecting the image in the other in the other in the other in the other . . .

"Herbert George Morley Roberts Wells, Esq." (1967): a story of anticipated stories written by and about an anticipator of other people's stories.

"Love That Universe" (1966): mankind, to save itself, must think nice thoughts in unison.

"Crusade" (1966): a purely mechanical intelligence conceives of animate intelligence on Earth—and launches a vendetta against it; told from the mechanical intelligence's point of view.

"The Cruel Sky" (1967): the crippled inventor of a levitation machine and his assistant are caught in the air in a Himalayan storm.

"Neutron Tide" (1970): a famous joke story leading up to a real groaner of a pun.

"Transit of Earth" (1970): a stranded astronaut prepares himself to die alone on Mars, but records the symbolic simultaneous sunrise and sunset visible when Earth passes in front of the sun.

"A Meeting with Medusa" (1971): a cyborg explores Jupiter in a balloon and discovers huge life forms.

BIBLIOGRAPHY OF NON-FICTION

This alphabetical listing simply records first editions of the most significant volumes by Clarke devoted primarily to non-fiction. Some of these works are pure scientific exposition, others are personal speculations, some contain memoir material, and some contain previously discarded items of fiction. *The Lost Worlds of 2001*, for example, contains materials excised from *2001* as well as entries from Clarke's diary kept while collaborating with Kubrick. Many of these books reprint Clarke's magazine articles of science and speculation. Hence, for those interested in Clarke's non-fiction, these volumes will supply a true cross-section of his voluminous production.

Beyond Jupiter, with Chesley Bonestell. Boston: Little Brown, 1972.
Boy Beneath the Sea, with Mike Wilson. New York: Harper, 1958.
The Challenge of the Sea. New York: Holt, Rinehart; London: Muller, 1960.
The Challenge of the Spaceship: Previews of Tomorrow's World. New York: Harper, 1959; London: Muller, 1960.
The Coast of Coral. New York: Harper; London: Muller, 1956.
The Exploration of Space. New York: Harper; London: Temple, 1951. revised edition, New York: Harper, 1959.
The Exploration of the Moon, with R. A. Smith. London: Muller, 1954; New York: Harper, 1955.
The First Five Fathoms: A Guide to Underwater Adventure, with Mike Wilson. New York: Harper, 1960.
First on the Moon, with the Apollo 11 astronauts. Boston: Little Brown, 1970.
Going into Space. New York: Harper, 1954; as *The Young Traveler in Space,* London: Phoenix House, 1954.
Indian Ocean Adventure, with Mike Wilson. New York: Harper, 1961; London: Barker, 1962.
Indian Ocean Treasure, with Mike Wilson. New York: Harper, 1964.
Interplanetary Flight: An Introduction to Astronautics. London: Temple, 1950; New York: Harper, 1951; revised edition, London: Temple; New York: Harper, 1958.
Into Space, with Robert Silverberg. New York: Harper, 1972.
The Lost Worlds of 2001. New York: New American Library, 1972.
The Making of a Moon: The Story of the Earth Satellite Program. New York: Harper; London: Muller, 1957; revised edition, New York: Harper, 1958.
Man and Space, with the editors of *Life.* New York: Time, 1964.
Profiles of the Future: An Inquiry into the Limits of the Possible. New York: Harper; London: Gollancz, 1962.
The Promise of Space. New York: Harper; London: Hodder and Stoughton, 1968.
The Reefs of Taprobane: Underwater Adventures Around Ceylon. New York: Harper; London: Muller, 1957.
Report on Planet Three. New York: Harper, 1972.
The Treasure of the Great Reef, with Mike Wilson. New York: Harper; London: Barker, 1964.
The View From Serendip. New York: Random House, 1977.
Voices Across the Sea. New York: Harper; London: Muller, 1958.
Voices from the Sky: Previews of the Coming Space Age. New York: Harper, 1965; London: Gollancz, 1966.

SELECTED, SECONDARY BIBLIOGRAPHY*
(with the assistance of Roger C. Schlobin)

Beja, Morris. "*2001*: Odyssey to Byzantium." *Extrapolation*, 10 (May 1967), 67–8. Rpt. in *SF: The Other Side of Realism: Essays on Modern Fantasy and Science Fiction*. Ed. Thomas D. Clareson. Bowling Green, OH: Bowling Green University Popular Press, 1971, pp. 265–67. Suggests that the protagonist of *2001*, David Bowman, duplicates the journey in William Butler Yeats' "Sailing to Byzantium." For reactions, see Alex Eisenstein and Robert Plank below.

Berstein, Jeremy. "Out of the Ego Chamber." *New Yorker*, 9 August 1969, pp. 40–65. This extensive "profile" is the most detailed study of Clarke. It is quite knowledgeable about both the man and his writing and is the only source cited by Clarke himself.

Byrnes, Asher. "Adventure on the Moon." *New Republic*, 23 October 1961, pp. 25–26. Lauds Clarke's *A Fall of Moondust* as a realistic exploration of scientific problems.

Clareson, Thomas D. "The Cosmic Loneliness of Arthur C. Clarke." In *Voices for the Future: Essays on Major Science Fiction Authors.* Vol. I. Ed. Thomas D. Clareson. Bowling Green, OH: Bowling Green University Popular Press, 1976, pp. 216–237, 278–280. Rpt. in *Arthur C. Clarke*. Ed. Joseph D. Olander and Martin Harry Greenberg. New York: Taplinger, 1977, pp. 52–71. A survey of Clarke's fiction that explores the themes of a renaissance in space for mankind and the "cosmic loneliness" occasioned by the wait for this intellectual culmination.

—————. "The Early Novels." *Algol*, 12, No. 1 (1974), 7–10. An examination of the overwhelming theme of the attractiveness of space in *Prelude to Space, Earthlight, A Fall of Moondust, The Sands of Mars, Against the Fall of Night,* and *The Lion of Comarre.* Also includes a discussion of the influence of Olaf Stapledon.

Eisenstein, Alex. "The Academic Overkill of *2001*." In *SF: The Other Side of Realism: Essays on Modern Fantasy and Science Fiction.* Ed. Thomas D. Clareson. Bowling Green, OH: Bowling Green University Popular Press, 1971, pp. 267–271. Responding to Beja and Plank (see above and below), Eisenstein criticizes both of their approaches and elaborates on the importance of the symbols of and allusions to God in *2001*.

Gillings, Walter. "The Man from Minehead." *Algol*, 12, No. 1 (1974), 12–14. A history of Clarke's short-story career with a chronological list of his stories current to 1967.

*Portions of this bibliography are endebted to Thomas D. Clareson's *Science Fiction Criticism: An Annotated Checklist* (Kent State University Press, 1972) and Roger C. Schlobin and Marshall B. Tymn's "The Year's Scholarship in Science Fiction and Fantasy" in its book cumulation for 1972–1975 (Kent State University Press, 1979) and its continuing annual installments in *Extrapolation* 1976–   ).

Hoch, David G. "Mythic Patterns in *2001: A Space Odyssey.*" *Journal of Popular Culture,* 4 (Spring 1971), 961–65. An analysis of *2001* using Joseph Campbell's *The Hero with a Thousand Faces* that focuses on rites of passage and the protagonist's final confrontation with the symbol (the monolith) of "the father."

Hollow, John. "*2001* in Perspective: The Fiction of Arthur C. Clarke." *Southwest Review,* 61 (1976), 113–28. Considers the ending of *2001* in light of Clarke's other fiction and concludes that Stanley Kubrick conceived the ending of the film since it is atypical of the usual ambiguous endings of most of Clarke's fiction.

Huntington, John. "The Unity of *Childhood's End.*" *Science Fiction Studies,* 1 (1974), 154–64. Rev. version as "From Man to Overmind: Arthur C. Clarke's Myth of Progress." in *Arthur C. Clarke.* Ed. Joseph D. Olander and Martin Harry Greenberg. New York: Taplinger, 1977, pp. 211–22, 234–35. Stressing *Childhood's End,* this is a discussion of Clarke's vision of mankind's two-step evolution from the rational to the transcendental.

Lehman-Wilzig, Sam N. "Science Fiction as Futurist Prediction: Alternate Visions of Heinlein and Clarke." *The Literary Review,* 20 (1976), 133–51. Contrasts the fictions of Robert A. Heinlein and Clarke to demonstrate that good science fiction offers a profitable vision of future social forms and political institutions.

Leiber, Fritz. "Way-Out Science." *National Review,* 9 April 1963, pp. 289–91. Commends Clarke's *Profiles of the Future,* along with Sir Bernard Lovell's *Exploration of Outer Space,* as a meaningful confrontation with the immenseness of space.

Moskowitz, Sam. "Arthur C. Clarke." In *Seekers of Tomorrow: Makers of Modern Science Fiction.* Cleveland: World, 1966. Rpt. Westport, CT: Hyperion, 1974, pp. 374–91. A biographic and literary survey of Clarke's career through the early 1960's.

Moylan, Tom. "Ideological Contradictions in Clarke's *The City and the Stars.*" *Science-Fiction Studies,* 4 (1977), 150–57. Criticizes Clarke's novel as an example of "bourgeois ideology."

Olander, Joseph D., and Martin Harry Greenberg, eds. *Arthur C. Clarke.* New York: Taplinger, 1977. This volume of essays by numerous critics is nearly as voluminous as all other Clarke criticism combined. About half the essays are devoted to major works and about half to considerations of his fiction as a whole. This is the best single source of textual criticism, and it includes a fairly complete primary bibliography, which includes original magazine publications, and a cursory secondary bibliography. Contents: "Introduction" by Olander and Greenberg, "Three Styles of Arthur C. Clarke" by Peter Brigg, "The Cosmic Loneliness of Arthur C. Clarke" by Thomas D. Clareson (see above), "The Outsider from Inside: Clarke's Aliens" by E. Michael Thron, "Of Myths and Polyominoes: Mythological Content in Clarke's Fiction" by Betsy Harfst, "Sons and Fathers in A.D. 2001" by Robert Plank, "Expectation and Surprise in *Childhood's*

End" by Alan B. Howes, "Contrasting Views of Man and the Evolutionary Process: *Back to Methuselah* and *Childhood's End"* by Eugene Tanzy, *"Childhood's End:* A Median Stage of Adolescence?" by David N. Samuelson (see below), and "From Man to Overmind: Arthur C. Clarke's Myth of Progress" by John Huntington (see above).

Ower, J. B. "Manacle-forged Minds: Two Images of the Computer in Science Fiction." *Diogenes,* No. 85 (1974), pp. 47–61. An analysis of the extrapolated computers and cybernetics and their fearful character in Harlan Ellison's "I Have No Mouth, and I must Scream" and Clarke's *2001.*

Plank, Robert. "1001 Interpretations of *2001." Extrapolation,* 11 (December 1969), 23–24. Rpt. in *SF: The Other Side of Realism: Essays on Modern Fantasy and Science Fiction.* Ed. Thomas D. Clareson. Bowling Green, OH: Bowling Green University Popular Press, 1971, pp. 265–67. An answer to Beja (see above) that emphasizes the necessary ambiguity in art and suggests a number of possible interpretations of *2001.* Also see Eisenstein above.

Rogers, Robert. "The Psychology of the 'Double' in *2001." Hartford Studies in Literature,* 1 (1969), 34–36. Criticizes the lack of the presence of man's intellect and rationality in the film version of *2001.*

Samuelson, David N. *"Childhood's End:* A Median Stage in Adolescence?" *Science-Fiction Studies,* 1 (1973), 4–17. Rev. version in *Arthur C. Clarke.* Ed. Joseph D. Olander and Martin Harry Greenberg. New York: Taplinger, 1977, pp. 196–210, 232–34. Examines *Childhood's End* and concludes that, while it embodies some of the characteristics of the best science fiction, it is flawed by its dichotomy between the goals of myth and science.

————. "Studies in the Contemporary American and British Science Fiction Novel." Ph.D. dissertation, University of Southern California, 1969. Rpt. as *Visions of Tomorrow: Six Journeys from Outer to Inner Space.* New York: Arno, 1975. Includes a thorough analysis of *Childhood's End.*

Scholes, Robert, and Eric S. Rabkin. *Science Fiction: History, Science, Vision.* New York: Oxford University Press, 1977. Contains a critical reading of *Childhood's End.*

Slusser, George Edgar. *The Space Odysseys of Arthur C. Clarke.* San Bernardino, CA: Borgo Press, 1978. A survey of Clarke's work from his literary beginnings in the 1930's to *Imperial Earth* in 1976.

Smith, Godfrey. "Astounding Story! About a Science Fiction Writer." *New York Times Magazine,* 6 March 1966, pp. 28, 75–77. An examination of the epic scope of *2001* and *Childhood's End,* which includes a biographical survey.

Sutton, Thomas C., and Marilyn Sutton. "Science Fiction as Mythology." *Western Folklore,* 28 (October 1969), 230–37. This examination of the mythic and mythopoetic in science fiction contains an extended analysis of Clarke's "The Star," which concludes that it is one of the best mythopoetic mixtures of myth and religion, human nature, and technology.

Watson, Ian. Review of *The Fountains of Paradise*. *Foundation*, No. 17 (1979), pp. 75–77. Clarke's newest and last novel is still too new to have generated any criticism. This is the best of the early reviews. Watson comments sensitively on the novel's stylistics, structure, major themes of the natures of man and God, ideology, and technology.

BIBLIOGRAPHIC NOTE

There are also a number of general works on science fiction that comment on Clarke and his writings; in fact, it is unusual to find one that doesn't. Among the more important are the Clarke bibliographies in L. W. Currey's *Science Fiction and Fantasy Authors: A Bibliography of First Printings of Their Fiction* (Boston: G. K. Hall, 1979), R. Reginald's *Science Fiction and Fantasy Literature: A Checklist, 1700–1974, with Contemporary Science Fiction Authors II* (2 Vols. Detroit: Gale Research, 1979), and Donald H. Tuck's *The Encyclopedia of Science Fiction and Fantasy Through 1968* (2 Vols. Chicago: Advent, 1974, 1978). Critical and biographical items of note are contained in Brian W. Aldiss' *Billion Year Spree: The History of Science Fiction* (London: Weidenfeld & Nicolson, 1973), James Gunn's *Alternate Worlds: The Illustrated History of Science Fiction* (Englewood Cliffs, NJ: Prentice-Hall, 1975), David Ketterer's *New Worlds for Old: The Apocalyptic Imagination, Science Fiction, and American Literature* (Bloomington and London: Indiana University Press, 1974), and Donald A. Wollheim's *The Universe Makers: Science Fiction Today* (New York: Harper & Row, 1971). Of particular note are the six excellent essay-reviews in the five-volume *Survey of Science Fiction Literature: Five Hundred 2,000-Word Essay Reviews of World-Famous Science Fiction Novels with 2,500 Bibliographical References* (Ed. Frank N. Magill. Englewood Cliffs, NJ: Salem Press, 1979): *"Childhood's End"* by David N. Samuelson (I, 337–41), *"The City and the Stars"* by Jack Williamson (I, 374–77), *"Imperial Earth"* by Donald L. Lawler (III, 1019–25), *"Rendezvous with Rama"* by William H. Hardesty III (IV, 1759–63), "The Short Fiction of Arthur C. Clarke" by Gary K. Wolfe (IV, 1926–29), and *"2001: A Space Odyssey"* by George Slusser (V, 2343–49).

INDEX

This is a subject, name and title index. Titles by Clarke are entered as main items; titles by others are listed under the names of the respective authors.